ASPERGER'S RULES!

HOW *to* MAKE SENSE *of* SCHOOL *and* FRIENDS

by BLYTHE GROSSBERG, PsyD

Magination Press
Washington, DC
American Psychological Association

Published by
MAGINATION PRESS
An Educational Publishing Foundation Book
American Psychological Association
750 First Street, NE
Washington, DC 20002

For more information about our books, including a complete catalog, please write to us, call 1-800-374-2721, or visit our website at www.apa.org/pubs/magination.

Printed by Worzalla, Stevens Point, Wisconsin
Book design by Oliver Munday

Library of Congress Cataloging-in-Publication Data

Grossberg, Blythe N.
Asperger's rules! : how to make sense of school and friends / by Blythe Grossberg. p. cm.
Includes bibliographical references.
ISBN 978-1-4338-1128-9 (hardcover : alk. paper) —
ISBN 978-1-4338-1127-2 (pbk. : alk. paper)
1. Autism in children. 2. Autistic children—Education.
3. Asperger's syndrome—Social aspects. I. Title
RJ506.A9G758 2012
618.92'85882—dc23

Manufactured in the United States of America

10 9 8 7 6 5 4 3 2 1

CONTENTS

CONTENTS

CHAPTER 1

INTRODUCTION

Though they are very smart and talented, kids with Asperger's sometimes struggle in school. They often have a hard time understanding other people, particularly when people don't state exactly what they mean. If you share some traits with Asperger's kids, or if you have Asperger's, you may find yourself in the strange situation of having a lot of information about a subject at school, or an opinion about something being discussed in class, but not being able to figure out a way to tell your teacher about your ideas. Your classmates may have an easier time getting teachers to listen and understand what they are trying to explain. That is because they know certain ways to act and rules for communicating that are not spoken or written down. Kids with Asperger's sometimes have a more difficult time understanding these unwritten rules, and may feel frustrated and misunderstood.

Everyone has to learn rules of behavior because these rules help school—and life—run well. In some ways, school is like a board game. If there are no rules, people simply can't play the game in a way that makes sense to them and others. While other kids may seem to understand the rules without having them explained, kids with Asperger's may have to learn and review the rules more directly. This doesn't mean that kids with Asperger's are less intelligent. It's just the way they learn. This book will explain these rules to you and help you set goals about learning and following these rules.

Learning the rules is an important part of school. In fact, a large part of school isn't just taking tests, reading books, and writing. Instead, it's learning how to communicate with your teachers and friends in a way that helps them understand you and that lets them know you understand them. While this part of school isn't graded, it's nevertheless very important. If you can understand what your teachers want and expect from you, you will be better able to show your true talents in school.

This book makes school easier for kids like you by explaining the confusing—and often unexplained—rules of the classroom. It will help you understand your teachers and their expectations, even the expectations of you they don't state out loud. You will learn how to understand your feelings and handle uncomfortable emotions. You

> This book helps you understand all the rules of the classroom, even those the teacher doesn't state outright.

> Learning the rules of behavior is an important part of school.

will learn rules and behaviors to help you have an easier time with teachers, friends, and classmates, and you will acquire **strategies** to make your schoolwork easier to do and understand. You will learn rules for hanging out with other kids and dealing with bullies. You will learn more about your talents and how to use them to your advantage in school. Finally, you will learn how to maintain healthy habits to help you feel good.

Not all of the examples used in the book will apply to your life, and that's okay. Once you get comfortable with the rules in this book, you will be able to apply them to many different situations.

This book helps you **decipher** that other part of school—the part that the teachers don't always talk about but that is critical to how you feel and perform at school. Using this book will help you understand the rules at school, even those that are never written down. Subjects covered in the book include:

➤ Rules to understand teachers, classmates, and friends.

➤ Rules to feel valuable and comfortable in school.

➤ Rules to communicate and make friends with other kids.

➤ Rules to develop and use your talents.

HOW THIS BOOK WORKS

Each chapter in this book will cover a specific part of life—including the **rules** of the classroom, ways to get along with classmates, and how to work with teachers. Each chapter will explain the rules about how that area of school works and then help you **brainstorm** ways in which you can improve in that area and give you a chance to practice those ways. Finally, you will come up with reachable and realistic goals for yourself related to that area. **Goals** are steps you can take, with the help of your parents, teachers, counselors, and friends, to improve in a certain area.

While reading this book, consider yourself a scientist who tries out new ideas or formulas in the laboratory and then sees how well they

GLOSSARY

strategy:
a way of doing things that helps you use your skills and that can make the task easier and more comfortable for you.

decipher:
To figure something out, such as a code or other people's behavior that may at first appear confusing.

rule:
An accepted way of doing something. There are many rules about students' behavior in schools.

brainstorm:
a problem-solving technique that involves a person or group coming up with ideas about how to solve a problem or accomplish a goal.

goal:
an idea about the progress or achievement you would like to make in a certain area. Goals can be long- or short-term.

work. Don't be afraid to try something new. After all, that's the process that scientists use to come up with a new idea or invention. After you try something new, you will think about how it worked or didn't work, and what you need to do differently in the classroom.

RECOGNIZING YOUR TALENTS

Before we discuss rules and goals, take a moment to think about your strengths. You have a lot of great talents that you should understand and appreciate. Now is a good time for you to sit back and think about your unique skills and traits. What are your top five talents—the qualities you possess that make you special?

My Top Five Talents

1. _____

2. _____

3. _____

4. _____

5. _____

You can write about qualities you have, such as "I am kind to animals," "I am responsible about doing my chores," or "I am nice to little kids." You can also write about talents you have, such as "I'm good at building with Legos," "I'm creative in designing paper airplanes," "I can write creative songs," or "I know a lot about Medieval history."

Even though you have a great deal of talents, you may also recognize areas that you would like to improve. Throughout this book, you will set goals for yourself—things that you would like to change or achieve. Setting goals does not mean that you are in any way wrong or bad or lacking talent. You are already talented, so setting goals doesn't mean that you can't keep the talents you already have. Instead, designing goals is about helping yourself feel better and more comfortable at school—with other kids, with teachers, and with yourself.

MAKING SMART GOALS

Just like a scientist devising an experiment, you will need to figure out exactly what you want to accomplish and how to go about it. One way to do this is to first create a **SMART** goal. Think of a **SMART** goal as following a specific formula, where S stands for **Specific**, M for **Measurable**, A for **Attainable**, R for **Realistic**, and T for **Timely**. So, the first step is to come up with a **Specific** goal, one that completely describes what you want and how you might get it. Consider the following goals:

➤   I want to make more friends.

This is not very specific. The goal doesn't state how you are going to make more friends or where you would find more friends.

➤   I want to join the drama club, so I can make more friends.

This goal is very specific. It states exactly how you are going to make more friends.

Now, the next step in making a **SMART** goal is to make the goal **Measurable**. This means you should include a quantitative indicator or due date so you can determine if and when you have achieved the goal. For instance:

➤   I would like to do better with my homework.

This is not a measurable goal. How would you measure "better"? What do you mean by "better"? Are you trying to get a higher grade or finish your homework on time?

So, how could you change this goal into something that is more measurable? How about something like this?

➤   I would like to improve handing in my homework so I'm only missing one assignment or fewer this month.

This goal is very measurable. You will know if you achieve it, because you can easily count the number of assignments you miss in a month.

How about the A in **SMART**? This refers to **Attainable**, or reachable. For example:

➤   I would like to be president of my school.

You might be a great candidate, but this goal may or may not be attainable because there are a lot of other people running.

To make the goal more attainable, you could change it to something like this:

➤   I would like to run for president, even if I don't win.

This goal is attainable, as you can always run for president, even if you don't win the election.

Attainable is related to the idea of R, or **Realistic**. While it is good to challenge yourself, your goal should be something you are reasonably able to accomplish with the resources available to you. Take a look at the following goals:

➡ I would like to write a research paper that figures out what went wrong with the *Challenger* space shuttle.

Instead, how about this example:

It may not be realistic to figure out this problem because you don't have access to the information at NASA or the training to solve the problem yourself.

➡ I would like to write a research paper that discusses what scientists think were some of the problems that may have resulted in the *Challenger* space shuttle explosion of 1986 and offer my own theories of what went wrong.

This is a realistic goal, because you can use the resources in the library to find out what scientists who have studied the Challenger *explosion think.*

Lastly, there's the T in **SMART**, which stands for **Timely**. That means that you want your goals to be achievable within a realistic time frame and relate to things that are important now. How timely do you consider the following goal?

➡ I would like to be a professional writer.

While this is a great goal, you don't need to worry about it until you are an adult.

Instead, try this:

➡ I would like to improve my essay writing skills this year in school.

LOOKING AT YOUR GOALS

This is a timely goal, as it relates to something you need to work on now.

At the end of each chapter, you will be given an opportunity to develop your goals. As you are setting each goal, remember to assess how SMART it is—that is, how Specific, Measurable, Attainable, Realistic, and Timely it is. You can look in the section above if you need help remembering how to set SMART goals. Or ask your parents. The goals are yours to choose, and can be whatever you want them to be. You may stick with the idea of the goal, such as "I want to make new friends at school," but change it so that it is more Specific or Attainable, such as, "I will join the robotics club or attend a camp this summer so I can meet new kids."

As you set goals, write down your top three goals on a piece of paper. It might help to stick them on your bulletin board or tape them to your mirror to remind you of what you want to accomplish.

You can go on to do great things, but remember—long journeys start with a single step. Start with SMART goals, and you will realize your great potential. Have a fun and interesting trip!

CHAPTER ❷

YOUR FEELINGS *and* EMOTIONS

This chapter is about how to make sense of what you feel. It's completely normal to feel upset, angry, and overwhelmed, just as it's normal to feel happy. This chapter will help you understand and identify when you might be starting to feel overwhelmed and will help you come up with some ideas about how best to handle this type of feeling.

GLOSSARY

TEST YOURSELF:
How Well Do You Understand What You Feel?

1 . How do you recognize if you are feeling upset in class?

__a. I don't realize I'm upset until it's too late.

__b. I am sometimes a bit shaky or uncomfortable, but I don't do much about it.

__c. I know how to take deep breaths or go for a walk if I feel I am getting angry or upset in class.

2. What makes you feel happy at school?

__a. I am not sure what makes me feel happy.

__b. I feel happy sometimes, but I'm not sure why.

__c. I understand that working in my area of interest (which may be math, computers, art, history, or another area) makes me feel the happiest at school.

3. How do you calm down if you are upset in the classroom?

__a. I am not sure how to calm down.

__b. I try to calm down, but often, I get really upset.

__c. I have worked on ways to calm down, such as taking deep breaths and imagining myself in a calm place.

4. What do you do when you are feeling overwhelmed?

__a. I often say and do things I don't mean.

__b. I try to concentrate on something else.

__c. I've arranged with my teacher to take a walk away from other kids.

5. Do you understand what makes your friends happy?

__a. I am not sure what makes my friends happy.
__b. My friends are happy when I am happy.
__c. I understand some of the games and activities that my
friends like.

If you answered mostly "a," you may need some help, as many people do, recognizing your emotions and those of others. You may also need to identify when you are starting to feel stressed out and learn how to handle these situations. This chapter can help you start to understand yourself a little bit more.

If you answered mostly "b," you understand some of what you and other people feel, and you have some good strategies to help yourself deal with change. Read on in this chapter to figure out how to make these strategies more effective.

If you answered mostly "c," it sounds like you understand what you feel and how to deal with the uncomfortable emotions everyone feels at times. Read on to find out if there are some other strategies that might help you but that you might not yet have thought about.

UNDERSTANDING WHAT YOU FEEL

Sometimes people describe emotions as if they were colors. Red might represent anger, while blue feels like calm. You may experience the full rainbow of emotions—from red (angry) to pink (happy) to black (sad). You may have different colors you associate with these emotions; each person sees emotions in a different way. It's normal to experience a range of emotions, and some days are filled with different feelings. You may feel tired or grumpy when you get up, and then feel happy when you get to school and find that another kid brought a video game to play during recess. You may feel angry when you find that you forgot your homework but then feel peaceful when you go out into the sun at recess. Sometimes, you can feel more than one thing at once. For example, if you find out that your friend is moving away, you may feel sad because you will miss her, but you may also feel happy because she has invited you to visit.

It may help you understand how you feel if you can put a label or even a color on each of your emotions. Here are some of the many emotions you may feel regularly:

➦ Happy

➦ Calm

➦ Angry

➦ Upset

➦ Confused

➦ Embarrassed

➦ Nervous or worried

➦ Sad

➦ Lonely

Can you think of others?

You can also **visualize**, or imagine, your emotions, as parts of the rainbow, or as the different temperatures on a thermometer with mercury inside. When you are calm and happy, you can think about the thermometer being at the bottom level, but as you get angrier and more upset, the level of the thermometer rises. It may help to imagine your feelings this way so that you can understand what you are feeling and when you might be starting to feel upset.

visualize: to create a picture in your mind.

There are some emotions that you may know well. For example, how do the following situations make you feel?

➦ Getting a new present that you really want

➦ Seeing a good friend

➡   Petting a friendly dog

➡   Getting a good grade

➡   Learning about something that interests you

The situations above can make you feel good. What are some other situations that make you feel happy?

_____.

How do these situations make you feel?

➡   Being unsure about what to do in class.

➡   Not being able to find your friends at lunch.

➡   Getting a bad grade.

➡   Hearing someone say something mean about you.

These are usually situations that involve feeling lonely, sad, confused, or hurt, and they may make you feel especially bad if your day is already not going well or you are feeling unsure of yourself.

What are some other situations that make you feel sad?

_____.

What are some situations that make you feel angry?

_____.

Are there situations that make you feel two things at once, such as sad and angry?

_____.

LISTENING TO YOUR BODY

Your body provides you with clues about how you are feeling.

If you are not sure what your emotions are telling you or why you feel the way you do, your body will often give you some clues.

Here are some signals from your body that you are feeling good:

➤ Your muscles are relaxed.

➤ Your breathing is calm and easy.

➤ You are neither too hot nor too cold.

➤ You are not hungry or thirsty.

➤ You are well-rested.

➤ You are not sweaty (unless it's warm outside, and the heat makes you sweat).

Here are some signals from your body that you are feeling bad:

➤ Your muscles are tight.

➤ You have a headache.

➤ You have a stomach ache.

➤ You are breathing rapidly.

➤ You are faint, or light-headed.

➤ You are sweaty.

➤ You are cold or heated.

➤ You feel like you are about to lose control.

➤ You are clenching your fists.

How does your body tell you that you are happy?

_____.

How does your body tell you that you are upset?

_____.

UNDERSTANDING HOW OTHER PEOPLE FEEL

It is hard to understand how other people feel, but it's often easier if you start by asking yourself, "how would I feel in this situation?" For example, if you were insulted by another kid, you would probably feel upset, hurt, and angry. Other people are no different. They most likely would feel the same way you do in that situation.

rule of thumb: a general principle not intended to be strictly applicable to every situation.

Here's a general **rule of thumb:** to understand how other people feel, think about how you would feel in the same situation.

People may also give you a clue about how they feel if you observe their body language, or how they hold themselves and what they do with their bodies.

Here are some signs that someone may be angry, bored, or upset:

➤ His face may be red.

➤ He may look away from you.

➤ He might be crying or have tears in his eyes.

➤ He may be hunched over or not stand straight.

➤ He may be crossing his arms.

➤ He may narrow his eyes.

➤ He may be yelling, raising his voice, or speaking quickly.

The next time your teacher or parents get upset, observe their body language. You will learn how to identify immediately when people are upset by watching what they do with their bodies.

PUT YOUR KNOW-HOW TO WORK

Practice Identifying Emotions

You can practice identifying your own and other people's emotions just as you might practice identifying leaves, birds, or bugs.

During the day, you can practice deciphering your emotions. At a free moment, stop and ask yourself:

➤➤ How do I feel right now?

➤➤ How does my body feel now?

➤➤ Why do I feel this way?

➤➤ Is there anything I can do to make myself feel better right now, such as taking a deep breath or a short break?

When you read books, you can also practicing identifying the emotions of the characters. Ask yourself:

➤➤ How is the character in this book feeling now?

➤➤ Why does the character feel this way?

➤➤ How would I feel in this same situation?

You may want to keep a journal in which you record how you are feeling at that moment. You can record your emotions at different times of the day, such as when you get up, when you are in school, when you come home, and when you go to bed. If you look at your journal entries over a week or two, you may notice certain patterns. See if you can notice whether you regularly feel bad or good at the same times each day. If you practice identifying your emotions and those of others, even fictional characters in books, you will improve your ability to judge how you and others feel in common situations.

RANKING YOUR PROBLEMS

Now that you have learned some signs to recognize what you are feeling, you can begin thinking about strategies to deal with feelings that are uncomfortable or upsetting. One key to dealing with upsetting situations in the classroom is to rank them. This method may help you realize that problems that seem overwhelming in the moment probably aren't as serious as they first appear or feel. Consider the following levels:

Level-One Problem: This is a really minor problem, such as a kid yelling. It's annoying, but it goes away in a minute. It's not usually something to get too upset about, though loud noises can be upsetting.

Level-Two Problem: Okay, this is something a bit more major, like your teacher telling you that you have to re-do your work. It's annoying and may make you upset for a while, but it's not the end of the world.

Level-Three Problem: This kind of problem requires some work to fix. For example, you may need to work on getting picked for soccer during gym class. It's fixable, and totally doable, but you have to put your brain to work thinking about a solution, and you may need to work with other people, such as the gym teacher.

Level-Four Problem: This kind of problem is serious. It may involve getting hurt, such as falling down and injuring yourself. It's still fixable, but it's a hard problem to overcome. Fortunately, not many problems fall into this category.

Level-Five Problem: This type of situation affects a lot of people, such as a plane crash or tornado. Again, not many problems fall into this top-level category.

When you have a problem, take a moment and think about which number you would put on it. What level problem is it? By the way, different people can assign different numbers to a problem. Though this may seem confusing, it just means that one person may consider a problem a bit more serious (or less serious) than another person does. It is helpful to assign a level to a problem, because thinking about it in the context of other problems may help you see that it is not as serious as it seems at first. You may realize that many of the problems during the school day, such as a kid saying something annoying, are really level-one problems most of the time, though they seem much more important in the moment.

PUT YOUR KNOW-HOW TO WORK

Assign Levels to Problems

What level are the following problems? Rank them from one to five, with one being an easy problem to fix and five being a serious problem affecting a lot of people.

➡️ A friend telling you he can't come over today:___

➡️ Getting a bad grade on an essay:____

➡️ Not being selected for the team or play you wanted to be part of:___

➡️ Water damage that ruins books and computers in your school:___

➡️ A virus that affects a lot of people and makes them sick: ___

It's up to you which numbers you put on these problems, but your rankings should reflect that the problems listed above get more serious and higher in number as you go along.

DECODING YOUR FEARS

Feeling fearful is a normal part of life, and fears help you protect yourself. For example, the fear of heights is common, and it often protects people from getting themselves into dangerous situations.

However, sometimes we have fears that aren't realistic. For example, when we are in a loud place, we may fear that the walls are closing in on us, but that fear is only in our heads. You may talk yourself into feeling scared of things about which the fear is worse than the reality. Sometimes, what you tell yourself about a situation is much worse than reality.

For example, do you remember starting school when you were younger? You may have had fears and thoughts such as the following:

➤ My teachers will be mean to me.

➤ I won't make any friends.

➤ The kids will be mean.

➤ I won't know anything.

After a few days in your new school, you probably began to realize that these were just thoughts, not reality. Are there other fears that you once had that turned out not to be as bad as you once thought?

Sometimes, what makes our fears worse is the thoughts that we attach to them. We can look at the same exact situation in different ways—and our thoughts about the situation can make it better or worse. For example, here are some common situations and the thoughts we often have about them.

Situation: You are in a class in which you know no one.
Unhelpful way to look at the situation: No one here will like me.
Helpful way to look at the situation: I will have a chance to meet new people.

Situation: You received a "B" on a test.
Unhelpful way to look at the situation: I am so stupid. I should've gotten an "A."
Helpful way to look at the situation: I did really well on one part of the exam and will ask my teacher to review the other part.

Situation: You are going on a field trip to an unknown place.

Unhelpful way to look at the situation: I am so scared because I don't know anything about the museum where we are going.
Helpful way to look at the situation: I can handle this trip, even though it's unfamiliar. I've been on similar trips in the past, and I might enjoy looking at the exhibits in the museum.

When fears overcome us, we are often only looking at situations in an unhelpful way. If we take the time to consider the thoughts we have about the situation, we may realize that we are doing one of the following things:

➡ Thinking that everything is always going to turn out for the worse, though it doesn't often wind up that way. For example, we forget that although a field trip is sometimes scary, we might actually enjoy what we are going to see. Some of what we imagine about a situation, such as getting lost on a field trip, is very unlikely to happen, and if we take a moment and think about it, we may realize that our fears are unrealistic. When we assume the worst about a situation, it is called **"catastrophizing."** Can you think of other times when you assumed the worst about a situation?

➡ We might also forget the good parts of a situation, and we might forget what we did well and instead concentrate on what we didn't do as well. For example, if we get mostly good grades and then do badly on one test, we have a tendency to only concentrate on the bad grade instead of remembering all the times we did well. This is called **all-or-nothing thinking.** Can you think of times when you forgot to think about all parts of a situation, and you only thought about a situation in one way?

catastrophizing: thinking that something that isn't that bad is actually a disaster.

all-or-nothing thinking: when we think everything has to be one way and forget about anything in between; this type of thinking is also referred to as "black-and-white thinking" because it involves thinking about things as all black or all white, with nothing in between.

All-or-nothing thinking can cause us to fear future situations, because we start to concentrate only on the negative parts of a situation or the bad outcomes we've had in the past. For example, if you only think of the times you did badly on a test when you are taking another test, you might start to feel worried or fearful. However, if you also try to keep in mind the times when you did well, you might feel more confident and calmer.

When you are afraid of a situation or feeling badly about an event, ask yourself the following questions:

➤ Do I really need to feel worried or upset, or it is just the thoughts I am having, not reality? In other words, is the situation really bad, and is there another way I could think about it?

➤ What are some more helpful ways I might think about this situation?

➤ Am I using all-or-nothing thinking, or am I catastrophizing? Are there other ways to think about this situation?

DEALING WITH CHANGE

It is hard for everyone to deal with change. It's hard enough just dealing with every day at school, but when your teachers change the schedule, it's even more difficult. Change may make you feel scared or overwhelmed, but you may also find something new exciting. For example, if your teacher gives you a pop quiz, it may be very scary, but if your teacher suggests that everyone go outside and eat lunch, it may be a welcome change from eating in the cafeteria.

How can you best deal with the changes that sometimes occur in school? Have you tried any of the following strategies?

deep breathing: Taking a deep breath, counting to eight, and letting the air out slowly while counting to eight. Concentrate on the rising and falling of your tummy. You can place your hand on your stomach to feel your breath go in and out. Do this several times, and you will notice you feel a bit calmer. You can close your eyes for a minute if it helps you to feel calmer.

➤ Practice **deep breathing.** Concentrate on your breathing for a minute; this practice will give you a more relaxed state of mind in which to deal with the change. To practice deep breathing, breathe in deeply for eight counts, hold your breath for eight counts, and breathe out for eight counts. Feel your stomach rise and fall with your breath. You can practice this at any time, and, if you do it silently (which is very possible), you can even use deep breathing in class without your teacher or other students noticing.

➤ Ask your teacher what lies ahead, if possible, so you can know what to expect. You can also ask your teacher to provide you with advance notice of major changes in the daily routine, such as field trips or changes in the schedule.

➤ Try to think about what level problem the change is (to understand what level problem you have, see "Ranking Your Problems" on page 22). You may realize that the change is not as serious as you first thought.

➤ Try to notice how the other kids are reacting to the change. Perhaps work with a friend in your class, and follow her lead, if you know that this person can handle new situations well.

➤ Think about situations in the past when you had to deal with a change and handled it successfully and perhaps even enjoyed the new situation.

GETTING UPSET IN CLASS

Below are some common **triggers** or situations that may upset you in class and some ways that you might think about each trigger differently and deal with it more calmly and effectively. When you read over these common school situations that may make you upset, try to think about what level problem they are and whether or not they are serious in the long-term:

trigger
something that provokes you into getting upset.

Trigger (what makes you upset): You receive a bad grade on an assignment.
Helpful way to think about this situation: Perhaps a poor or lower-than-anticipated grade on an assignment is the teacher's way to help you improve and will give you motivation to work harder.
Ways to handle this situation: Try to meet with the teacher after class by speaking to her politely or sending her an e-mail (see the sample e-mail on page 52). Ask her how you can improve your work, and listen, without arguing, to the teacher's suggestions.

Trigger: A classmate makes a hurtful comment.
Helpful way to think about this situation: Sometimes, what may seem like a sarcastic or mean comment by a teacher or classmate wasn't intended to be so. Be sure to think about whether the comment was really meant to be hurtful, or whether the speaker might have just been trying to be funny.
Ways to handle this situation: If you feel that a student is continu-

ally making mean or sarcastic comments about you, ask the person privately to stop doing so (not in front of other people). If that doesn't work, you may need to ask your teacher to have this student stop his mean remarks.

Trigger: You feel overwhelmed by too much loud noise.
Helpful way to think about this situation: You may feel overwhelmed at the moment, but remind yourself that you will feel better if you can take a short break.
Ways to handle this situation: You might arrange in advance with your teacher to have a place to go when you are feeling overwhelmed. For example, will your teacher allow you a brief bathroom visit or trip to the water fountain? Ask to be excused from very loud events, such as fire drills, pep rallies, or loud concerts. It may not be possible to be excused from these events, so you can also wear some really small ear plugs (not headphones) that you insert into your ears and that other people can't see. You can also try to listen to some calming music with headphones, if you have a portable device such as an iPod. It's best to listen to headphones outside of the classroom, not in the classroom, as you want to appear respectful of your teacher and classmates. Some schools and teachers do not allow headphones, so be sure to check with your teacher ahead of time.

> There are helpful ways to think about your triggers so you can handle them calmly and effectively.

Trigger: Your teacher asks you to stop talking about a topic that interests you in class.
Helpful way to think about this situation: Consider that the teacher has a lot of material to cover, and there may not be enough time for you to talk about your area of particular interest, whether it's the Solar System, World War II, or *manga*. Consider whether the teacher is really out to get you, or just is trying to impose order and rules in the classroom.
Ways to handle this situation: Maybe you can arrange in advance to have a special sign, such as a tap on your shoulder, that the teacher can give you when you are getting too far off topic. See the teacher privately to discuss your area of interest with him or her in a more extensive way. Consider joining a club that addresses your area of interest so that you don't feel that you need to bring it up in the classroom.

Trigger: You have a special speaker in class, and you feel thrown off by the change in routine.

Helpful way to think about this situation: Think about other times you have had a change in routine, such as a field trip or assembly, and remind yourself that you handled it successfully and maybe even enjoyed it.

Ways to handle the situation: You may need to take a short break, for example by going to the bathroom. Work on some deep breathing exercises that you can use privately in the classroom to make you feel calmer and better. This means that when something upsets you, you take some very deep breaths and let them out through your nose. Concentrate on your breathing for a minute or two, and try to let go of some of your upset feelings and anger. Ask your teacher in advance when the rules of the classroom might change for the day. That way, you won't feel so thrown off by new events.

PUT YOUR KNOW-HOW TO WORK

Think About Your Triggers

Try to think about which triggers or situations upset you in you in the classroom, and consider some alternative ways you might think about each situation and some ways you might handle the situation differently.

My triggers are:

_____.

Here's what I do in response:

_____.

Here's what I might do differently:

_____

_____

_____.

KNOWING WHEN YOU NEED A BREAK

The first part of explaining when you need a break is to recognize on your own that you are getting overwhelmed or frustrated. Your body is like a car. It usually runs smoothly, but sometimes, your engine might start to overheat. In these cases, you need to pull over and give your engine—that is, your mind and body—a chance to cool down. It is important to catch yourself as your engine starts to overheat. If you allow yourself a moment to relax, you may be able to prevent yourself from getting totally overwhelmed. If you wait too long, it may be difficult to prevent your engine from getting overheated. How can you tell when you are getting overwhelmed? Think about some of the following signs:

➤➤ You are tired.

➤➤ You are hungry.

➤➤ You are feeling angry.

➤➤ You notice that you are getting red in the face or feel hot.

➤➤ You are feeling frustrated.

➤➤ You notice that your body is getting shaky.

➤➤ Your hands are sweaty.

Can you think of any other signs that you are getting overwhelmed?

_____

_____

_____.

A car's dashboard tells the driver that the car is overheated, has a flat tire, or needs more gas. You don't get these types of signs from your own body, but you do get other signs, like feeling tired, shaky, nervous, or sweaty. If you notice any of these signs, it may be time to take a break. Below are some strategies to help you cool down.

COOL DOWN

If you notice that you are feeling overwhelmed, what can you do?

Here are some ideas about how you can cool down:

➤➤ Practice deep breathing. Breathe in deeply, and pay attention to your breath as you breathe out. Repeat this several times, while resting your hands on your belly. You may want to close your eyes while doing this, if you can.

➤➤ Close your eyes and think about a calm scene, such as a lake, the ocean, or the woods.

➤➤ Ask your teacher if you can take a short walk to the bathroom or get a drink of water. You should work this arrangement out with your teacher ahead of time and only use it when you can't remain calm in the classroom. If possible, you want to be able to stay in the classroom and not miss out on anything.

➤➤ Ask your teacher if you can listen to music during recess or a break. Bring your iPod or another musical device to school with headphones, and store this device in a safe place until you need it. You may also want to have your name inscribed on the back of the device, in case you lose it.

You can practice strategies for cooling down, to be prepared for situations in school that make you feel anxious or stressed out.

➤➤ Look out the window for about a minute. Concentrate on something peaceful, like a tree or a cloud.

➤➤ Ask your teacher to wear a visor or hat if the lights of the classroom are overwhelming, unless wearing a hat or other head covering is against the rules at your school. A lot of classrooms have fluorescent lights that are very bright and overly stimulating.

➤➤ Ask your teachers to take a short walk during recess or lunch on the less crowded part of the playground or to sit for a while in the quiet library.

➤➤ Do some exercise outside the classroom, such as jumping jacks or wall push-ups.

PUT YOUR KNOW-HOW TO WORK

Plan Strategies for Cooling Down
Do you use any of these strategies below to help calm yourself
down? Mark each of these strategies with yes, no, or sometimes.

___Deep Breathing.

___Squeezing a soft, squishy toy in your hand.

___Trying to imagine that you are in a calm, peaceful place such as
in the woods, a garden, or at home in your room.

___Excusing yourself to take a walk or go to the bathroom or get a
drink. You might need to arrange this type of break in advance by
telling the teacher that you sometimes get upset and need a break in
class. Of course, you don't want to leave the classroom too often, or
you will miss out on the class material.

___With your teacher's permission, going out of the classroom and do-
ing some jumping jacks or wall push-ups, which involve planting your
hands about a foot apart on the wall and pushing off them until you
feel more relaxed.

___Visualizing, or imagining, a thermometer that is going down as you
slowly try to cool down.

Do you have any calming strategies that work for you?

_____

_____

_____

_____

_____

_____

➥ Try to imagine a gauge or thermometer going down as you cool down.

➥ Try to refrain from playing computer games on your cell phone or another device. This is not always a good way to calm down, as you may not always have your gaming device around, and your teachers and principal may not allow this kind of device in school.

➥ Try to figure out what level problem you are having, or how serious your problem is. Most problems are level-one problems, meaning that although they are very frustrating, they do not cause lasting problems or harm. Try to remember that your problem will be over soon.

Sometimes, it is hard to cool down, but you don't want to do anything that makes the problem worse. Here are some things you want to try to avoid when you are getting overwhelmed:

➥ Talking to other people, including friends and teachers, is a bad idea until you feel calmer. You may say things you don't mean. However, if you feel you can ask another person for help in a polite way, you should do so.

➥ Don't stay in a crowded room or area, if you can avoid it. You should remove yourself from other people, if possible.

➥ Don't express your anger in physical violence. Instead, try doing jumping jacks or running in place to get out some of your energy and frustration.

PREPARING A TALK WITH YOUR TEACHER

Now that you have figured out some of the causes or signs that you are upset and some of the ways you might cool down in the classroom, fill out this speech that you can use to ask your teacher to help you. You can send this to your teacher as an e-mail or letter or use it to speak with your teacher in person.

Dear Mr. or Ms._____:

(Fill in your teacher's subject here.)

I wanted to let you know a little bit more about the ways I sometimes behave in your classroom. As my parents told you, I have Asperger's syndrome. This means that while I try to behave in school and learn as much as I can, I sometimes get overwhelmed in your class. I don't want to get overwhelmed because I enjoy learning about _____. I notice that the things that sometimes make me feel upset are _____, _____, and _____.

(Fill in the blanks with your top two coping strategies or means of staying calm while staying in the classroom, such as breathing deeply or looking out the window.)

(Fill in the top three things that make you feel overheated here, such as group projects, lots of noise in the classroom, or a change in routine.)

(Mention what you will do here, such as "I will take a short walk and get some water. I will try to be back within two minutes.")

When I get upset, I will try to remain in the classroom and use _____ and _____ to calm down. However, sometimes, I may need to take a break by leaving the classroom. When I leave the classroom, I will _____. When I need to leave, I may give you a sign such as _____.

(Arrange a sign with your teacher, such as tapping your nose or ear.)

I very much appreciate your help. Please let me know if these sound like good ideas and what would work for you.

Thank you,

_____

(Fill in your name here.)

GETTING EXTRA HELP

Everyone has good and bad days, ups and downs. However, if the down days are far more plentiful than the good days, it might be time for you to talk to a parent, teacher, or another trusted adult, such as a religious leader, **counselor**, or family friend.

counselor: an adult, such as religious figure or therapist, who is trained to help people figure out ways to handle their problems.

Here are some signs that tell you that you might need to ask for help:

➤ You feel negative about yourself and your abilities.

➤ You feel isolated or alone.

➤ You feel that you can't get out of bed.

➤ You feel that you are worried all the time.

➤ You feel that you can't sleep well.

If you feel worried about yourself or feel down, please speak with a trusted adult and tell him or her how you feel.

GOAL SETTING:
FEELINGS RULES

Now that you've read the rules about understanding how you feel, write down some goals that you have. Make your goals SMART: that is, Specific, Measurable, Attainable, Realistic, and Timely. For example, here are some goals you might work towards:

➤ This week, I will try to figure out some ways to cool down when I start feeling overheated or overwhelmed.

➤ When I start to feel anxious or overwhelmed, I will take a minute to see how my body is feeling. If I can, I will take a short walk in school or outside of school.

➤ I will try speaking to my mother or father when I am feeling really upset and would like to find some ideas about how to calm down.

In this chapter, you have learned more about yourself: what you are feeling, the triggers that make you upset, and strategies to cool down if you get overwhelmed in the classroom. The next chapter will help you tell your teacher about yourself and help you work with your teacher to find the best ways to handle school.

CHAPTER 3

TEACHERS *and* ASKING FOR HELP

You may not realize that by asking your teachers for the right kind of help, you can make life a lot easier for yourself. To get help from your teachers, you have to understand your strengths and weaknesses. If you know the areas in which you need help, you can explain what you need, but you also have to understand that teachers have other kids to help, too. That means that you shouldn't take too much of their time. And be sure to thank your teacher for the help you receive.

TEST YOURSELF: How Well Do You Ask for Help?

1. What do your teachers know about you?
   __a. My teachers only know my name.
   __b. My teachers just think I am quiet.
   __c. My parents and I explained how I work to my teachers, and we work together with them.

2. How do you ask your teachers for help?
   __a. I don't ask my teachers for help.
   __b. I sometimes try to ask my teachers for help, but I have a hard time explaining what I need.
   __c. My teachers understand my strengths and weaknesses, and I regularly meet with them to work on material.

3. How do you thank your teacher for help?
   __a. I don't thank my teacher.
   __b. I want to thank my teacher, but I don't know how.
   __c. I thank my teacher and sometimes do favors for her, such as putting away books or helping other kids.

If you answered mostly "a," your teachers may not know you very well, and you may need to figure out better ways to ask your teachers for help and to explain yourself to them.

If you answered mostly "b," you are interested in getting help from your teachers to work better in class, which is great. Read on to find ways to approach your teachers and work with them.

If you answered mostly "c," you are doing a great job asking your teachers for help. Read this chapter to find ways you might tell them more about Asperger's and how you work best and to find ways to thank them for their help.

TELLING YOUR TEACHER ABOUT ASPERGER'S

One thing you need to decide is whether you tell your teacher that you are a kid with Asperger's. It's entirely up to you and your parents whether you decide to tell your teachers you have Asperger's syndrome. Here are some of the pros and cons of telling your teacher about Asperger's:

CONS (The reasons telling your teacher may be a bad idea)

➤➤ Your teacher may **stereotype** you, or think you are just like other people with Asperger's or like the idea of Asperger's she has in mind. For example, many people think everyone with Asperger's is good at math, but this isn't always true. If your teacher thinks you are like a stereotype, she may not really understand who you truly are.

➤➤ The teacher may or may not think you are a capable student if you share this information.

➤➤ The teacher may think you are using Asperger's to get around work.

PROS (The reasons why telling your teacher may be a good idea)

If your teachers know you have Asperger's, they may be more likely to understand your behavior and help you.

➤➤ Your teacher may have had experience with Asperger's before and may understand you better if you share this information with her. For example, she will understand why you might feel overwhelmed in crowds or in loud classrooms and will understand that you are not simply trying to be difficult.

➤➤ Your teacher can read more about Asperger's syndrome and learn about it, which will not only help you but also help other kids with Asperger's.

➤➤ If you provide the teacher with an informative handout on Asperger's, such as the one provided by OASIS (see the resources section at the end of the book for more information about how to get this handout, which explains what Asperger's is to teachers), the teacher will most likely understand that you are capable and that having Asperger's does *not* mean you can't be successful.

➤ Your teacher will understand why you may need special accommodations, such as breaks, if you have these types of help in school. In fact, if you have these types of help, your teacher may know that these supports are provided to you because you have Asperger's.

➤ If you approach her in the right way, she will understand that you are *not* trying to get around work but are interested in doing as well as you can and living up to your capabilities.

It is possible to tell your teachers what you need to succeed without mentioning that you have Asperger's. For example, you could say something such as the following:

➤ I find it hard to follow what is said during class, and I work best if you put information on the board. I will be sure to copy it into my notebook.

Explain your needs to your teacher.

➤ Sometimes, I need help organizing my work. Is it possible for me to meet with you during our free period just to review what I am doing?

Show your teacher that you are motivated and want to do well in class.

You should talk to your parents about whether or not you should reveal to your teachers (and to your classmates) that you have Asperger's. Don't let embarrassment be the reason you don't share this information. Well-informed people know that students with Asperger's are capable and smart.

EXPLAINING HOW YOU WORK IN SCHOOL

It may really help you get along better with your teachers if you explain to them at the beginning of the year how you work in school and how they can help you learn better and feel more comfortable in the classroom. Your teachers need to know that there are rules for understanding you too! For example, it may be hard for you sometimes to look people in the eye when you are speaking to them. This situation is very common for kids and even adults with Asperger's. A teacher who is unfamiliar with Asperger's may think you are not looking at him because you are rude or because you don't know any better. If your teacher knows it is simply difficult for you to look him straight in the eye, he will not assume that you are being impolite.

You can meet with your parents and teachers at the beginning of the year, or even at the end of the previous school year, to explain how you work best. You may want to rehearse and practice some of what you say beforehand.

You can (but don't have to) say things like the following:

➤➤ It's often hard for me to look people in the eye, but if you remind me to look at you with a special signal such as pointing to your eye, I will try to look you directly in the eye.

➤➤ I sometimes get overwhelmed if there is a lot of noise or lights or chaos in the classroom. Last year, my teacher allowed me to take a short walk, and then I returned to the classroom ready to work. Is this something I could try in your classroom? I can give you a signal, such as tapping my nose, that I need a short break.

➤➤ I sometimes forget to write down the homework. Is it possible for you to write it on the board at the beginning of class? Then, I will be sure to write it down and complete it the best I can.

➤➤ Sometimes, I find it hard to cope with changes in routine. I like everything to stay the same from day to day. It really helps me if I know about changes in the routine or schedule beforehand.

➤➤ I learn best by seeing things written down. Is it possible for you to write on the board? I find it hard to absorb everything just by listening.

Your teacher may have her own ideas about how to help you, and you should listen to these ideas, too, and accept that she may not always be able to do what you ask, since there are a lot of students in the class. However, if you tell the teacher at the beginning of the year or even before the year begins about how you work, you will most likely get along better with the teacher.

PUT YOUR KNOW-HOW TO WORK

Tell Your Teacher About Yourself
What are the top five things you want your teacher to know about you? Are there things that can help your teacher help you?

1. _____

2. _____

3. _____

4. _____

5. _____

FINDING INFORMATION FOR YOUR TEACHER

If you find that you are unable to explain yourself to your teacher, organizations such as OASIS (The Online Asperger's Syndrome Information and Support Center, http://www.aspergersyndrome.org) has handouts for teachers that explain the behavior and characteristics of many students with Asperger's syndrome. You can find these handouts on the web, and your parents can meet with your teachers and provide them with the handout. You can also use the handout and change it a bit to reflect what you feel is true about yourself. If you feel comfortable, you can read over the handout and use it to guide your conversation with your teacher about how your mind works and how you work best.

There are organizations, such as OASIS (http://www.aspergersyndrome.org/), on whose websites you can download basic fact sheets about Asperger's to show to your teachers.

THANKING YOUR TEACHER

You should be sure to thank the teacher for any help you receive, and you can also perhaps find ways to help your teacher. If you help your teacher, he will be more willing to help you.

Would you, for example, be able to do any of the following things to help your teacher?

➤➤ Teach kids who are struggling in an area you are good in, such as math, science, or history.

➤➤ Neaten up books in your classroom or school library.

➤➤ Erase the blackboards or clean the dry-erase boards.

➤➤ Give a presentation about an area you are interested in—whether it's explorers, dinosaurs, or lava—that adds to the class discussion of a topic.

ASKING FOR HELP WITH SCHOOL WORK

Occasionally, you may find that you need help with school work. Asking for help is not a form of weakness; instead, it is a form of strength. When you ask your teachers or coaches for help, you are telling them that you are interested in doing well in their class or activity and want to do better. You are showing them that you are confident enough to admit that you—like everyone at times—need help.

The first part of asking for help with school work is to realize when something is difficult for you. Even though you are smart, you may not understand everything presented to you in school—and you are not expected to. Do you have a sense of the areas that are difficult for you? If so, list them here:

Areas in which I need help:

1. _____

2. _____

3. _____

(List others if there are other areas in which you need help.)

Be sure to speak to your teacher respectfully, and be considerate of her time. (See Chapter 4 for more information about communicating with your teacher.) Here is an example of how you might ask your teacher for help with school work:

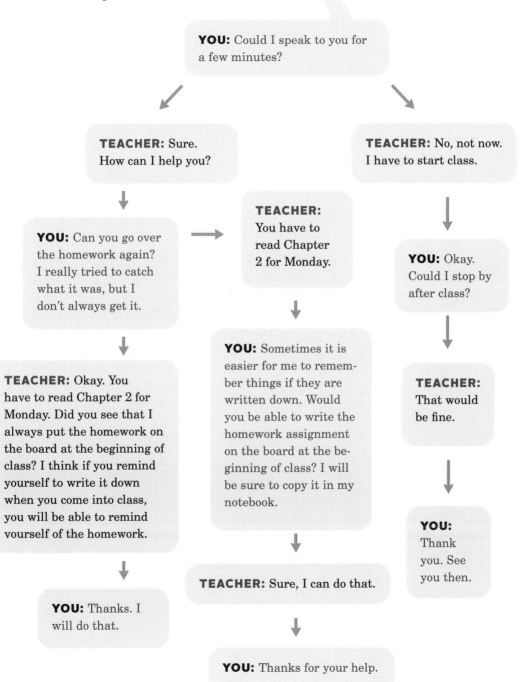

YOU: Could I speak to you for a few minutes?

TEACHER: Sure. How can I help you?

TEACHER: No, not now. I have to start class.

YOU: Can you go over the homework again? I really tried to catch what it was, but I don't always get it.

TEACHER: You have to read Chapter 2 for Monday.

YOU: Okay. Could I stop by after class?

TEACHER: Okay. You have to read Chapter 2 for Monday. Did you see that I always put the homework on the board at the beginning of class? I think if you remind yourself to write it down when you come into class, you will be able to remind yourself of the homework.

YOU: Sometimes it is easier for me to remember things if they are written down. Would you be able to write the homework assignment on the board at the beginning of class? I will be sure to copy it in my notebook.

TEACHER: That would be fine.

YOU: Thank you. See you then.

YOU: Thanks. I will do that.

TEACHER: Sure, I can do that.

YOU: Thanks for your help.

Your parents and other trusted adults, such as your grandparents, babysitters, and other relatives, are there to hug you after a long day (if you feel like a hug). They can help you figure out strategies, or new ways of doing things, and they can help you understand the other kids at school or a tough homework assignment. Remember, however, that you sometimes have to do things on your own. Parents are like the coaches who stand on the sides of football or basketball games. They help prepare you for the game (or school), and they can help you decide how to carry out a certain play. You can also talk with them when the game (or the school day) is over. During the school day, however, you have to make choices and interact with your teacher and your peers on your own. If you are having a difficult time, ask your parents to coach you through the situation. Here are some good ways you can prepare for school with your parents or other adults:

➽ You can practice what you are going to say in a conversation with another kid or a teacher.

➽ You can do a role-play, and your parents can play the part of the other person.

➽ You can talk about the best ways to handle a situation.

➽ You can discuss a difficult day with them and share your experiences.

➽ You can talk to them about your dreams and goals.

Here are some things that you should be doing on your own:

➽ If you want to make more friends or need to get help with your schoolwork, you should try to speak with other kids or teachers first. If you still have a difficult time, you can consult your parents. Before asking your parents to talk to teachers or other kids, try to have them coach you through a conversation.

➽ You should arrange your own get-togethers with friends by the time you are in middle school. Chapter 6 has advice on how to ask another kid over to your house. There are some helpful ideas about how to invite a kid over, what to say, and what to do while you are hanging out.

⤞ You should do your homework on your own. If you are confused about the assignment, you should ask your teacher. Your parents might also be able to explain how to approach the assignment if you are confused, but they shouldn't do your work for you.

⤞ You should start to keep an assignment book with your work listed for each night. Try to write down the assignments in class, and ask a teacher or friend for help if you miss something. You may also be able to use the school's website to find your assignments. If you are having trouble with this, it's all right to ask your parents, but find out how you can fill out your assignment book on your own. Ask your teacher or parent to show you how to use the website that lists your assignments, if there is one, and then start using this website on your own.

⤞ If your parents are packing your backpack or school bag every night, you should ask them to help you make a list of what you need. Eventually, you can follow the list and start packing your own bag. This task is good preparation for high school and being an adult, when you will have to pack your own stuff every day.

GOAL SETTING:
TEACHER RULES AND HELPING RULES

Now that you've read the rules about explaining yourself to teachers and asking for help, write down some goals that you have. Make your goals SMART: that is, Specific, Measurable, Attainable, Realistic, and Timely. For example, here are some goals you might work towards:

⤞ I will explain to my gym teacher how Asperger's affects me. I will talk to the teacher, looking him in the eye, explain that the noise during volleyball games bothers me, and ask to join the other kids who are jogging instead.

⤞ I will ask my teacher about what's going to happen during the holiday concert that is coming up so I know what to expect and feel more comfortable during the actual event.

➤ When my English teacher asks me to rewrite an essay, I will ask to meet with him so he can explain his comments to me. I will send him an e-mail that is polite and that asks when it's convenient for him to meet.

This chapter helped you figure out ways to approach your teacher for help. In the next chapter, you will learn more about the rules of the classroom that aren't written down but that your teacher expects you to follow.

CHAPTER 4

THE UNWRITTEN RULES *of the* CLASSROOM

Sometimes you might not be able to figure out what your teacher wants, but it's important to try to do so. There is a part of your grade that comes from being a good participant in classroom discussions and from acting fair and tolerant towards your teacher and classmates. If you disagree with the teacher, it's important to know how to talk to him or her with respect, even if you don't think the teacher is smart or kind.

In this chapter, you will read about the rules of the classroom that no one writes down, and you will learn how to participate in classroom discussions, which are an important part of middle school. You may often be too shy to participate, or you may find that you can't really pick up on what others are saying. You may also find that sometimes, you interrupt or annoy others without meaning to. But you have a lot to contribute to discussions in class, and this chapter will help you figure out how to join in the conversations that the teacher has with the class.

> A part of your grade has to do with respecting your teacher and understanding the rules of the classroom.

TEST YOURSELF:

How Well Do You Understand the Unwritten Rules of the Classroom?

1. During class discussions, do you:
   __a. interrupt your classmates to state your point of view.
   __b. yawn or act bored when your classmates don't understand things.
   __c. compliment your classmates' contributions.

2. If you receive a bad grade on a test, do you:
   __a. crumple up the paper because the teacher is obviously a moron for giving you a bad grade.
   __b. demand to have more of your teacher's time to review what you call the "boring stuff."
   __c. e-mail your teacher to politely ask to meet with him to talk about ways to improve on the next test.

3. If your teacher says you should write something down he is saying in class, do you:
   __a. ignore him.
   __b. write it down on your hand.
   __c. write it down in your notebook and put a star next to it.

4. When the teacher explains what you need to do in an essay to receive an "A," do you:

__a. tune out your teacher—it's not realistic for you hope to get an "A."

__b. listen to your teacher but then forget about what he said when writing your essay.

__c. write down what your teacher says and try to write your work accordingly.

5. When a teacher asks for neat work, do you:

__a. hand in the first handwritten draft you write.

__b. try to erase your mistakes or cross them out.

__c. type your work and look it over for errors.

If you answered mostly "a," you may be feeling confused about what your teachers want and expect from you. You may constantly be surprised by assignments that you think you understood but that the teacher returns to you with lower-than-expected grades. Read on to find out more about how you can put your talents to work and get the grades you have the potential to earn.

If you answered mostly "b," while you get the gist of your teachers' expectations, you may need to become a more attentive listener to your teachers' and classmates' needs and concerns. Read on to fine tune your understanding of the teachers' rules and language.

If you answered mostly "c," you are fairly adept at understanding what your teachers want and expect from you. Read on to find out if there is anything you hadn't known about deciphering, or decoding, your teachers' unwritten language.

CHECKING YOUR BODY LANGUAGE

In the classroom, your body language communicates a great deal about you. **Body language**, the way in which you use your body—your gestures, how you move, and your facial expressions—is like English or any other language. In fact, in some ways body language is even more important than what you say. Experts think anywhere from 60 to over 90% of communication between people is conveyed nonverbally. The gestures you use convey your meaning to the listen-

body language
The way in which you use your body to convey the meaning of what you say.

er. You can communicate to your teachers and your classmates exactly how you feel about something without even talking. For instance, these are signals that you are bored or disengaged:

This makes you appear so bored, you're falling asleep!

➤➤ yawning

➤➤ lying on your desk

➤➤ falling out of your chair

Although you may feel more comfortable looking at the floor, it conveys to people that you aren't interested in what they are saying.

➤➤ putting your fingers in your ears or covering your ears with your hands

➤➤ looking down at the floor

➤➤ scribbling randomly in your notebook or doodling

This may give the impression that you aren't paying attention.

➤➤ crossing your arms

➤➤ pulling a hood or hat over your face

Pulling your hood over your face conveys that you are trying to ignore the person talking to you.

Crossing your arms can make you look defensive or angry.

As you may notice, a lot of kids need to work on their body language, not just kids with Asperger's! In fact, most kids need to improve their body language. Here's how you might use your body language to show that you are interested and engaged (or being respectful of your classmates and teacher), even if you are not that interested in what is going on in the classroom:

➤➤ looking at the person who is talking, whether it's your teacher or classmates

➤➤ taking notes in your notebook or laptop while occasionally glancing up at the person talking, or glancing up when you are finished taking notes

While you might be trying to convey interest, standing too close can make some people uncomfortable.

➤➤ opening the book to the page you are studying

➤➤ sitting up in your chair

➤➤ maintaining the proper distance from people (about an arm's length)

➤   speaking loudly enough that other people can hear you, but not so loudly that it overwhelms them.

COMMUNICATING WITH YOUR TEACHER

It's important to speak with your teachers in polite ways that show you appreciate them. Remember, teachers will be more willing to help you if you act interested in what they say, and part of your grade is determined by your interaction with your teacher. Even if the teacher doesn't say directly that class participation and your interaction with the teacher are part of your grade, teachers may grade you a bit more easily if you are polite, likeable, and working hard in their class. Here are some strategies you can follow to help you get along with your teachers and communicate with them clearly and effectively.

RULES FOR ADDRESSING YOUR TEACHER

While your body language communicates a great deal about your meaning, *what* you say is important too. There are rules for polite communication.

If you follow these rules, you will show respect for your teacher:

➤   Say hello when you enter the classroom or see your teacher in other parts of the school and goodbye when class is dismissed. Try to look your teacher in the eye, meaning that you are focusing on his eyes, when saying hello and good bye.

➤   Say please and thank you.

➤   Ask for, don't demand, help, and thank your teacher for his help.

➤   Don't be too shy to ask for help—everyone needs help at times.

➤   Don't ever insult your teacher or the assignments.

➤   Don't question your teacher's intelligence.

There are ways to communicate with your teacher politely, whether talking or emailing, and you can improve your ways of doing so with practice.

- Show interest in the subject, even if it's not your favorite.

- Ask the teacher for help well in advance of the due date of an assignment or test.

- Give the teacher a few times when you can meet, in case he is busy during one of the times you would like to meet.

- Tell the teacher exactly how long you need from him to get help—and stick to it!

MORE WAYS TO COMMUNICATE WITH YOUR TEACHER

If you find it difficult to speak to your teacher directly, you can e-mail her. This form of communication may make it easier for you to communicate with teachers, but you still need to follow the rules of polite conversation.

Here is an example of a student's e-mail to a teacher asking for help. Note that the student addresses the teacher by her full name and does not begin the e-mail with "hey" or "hi." In addition, the e-mail follows the rules above.

Good! Addresses the teacher politely and by name.

Dear Ms. Smith,
I have some questions about the history research paper due next week. I am wondering if you have free time during lunch on Tuesday or Wednesday for us to meet for ten minutes so that I can show you my rough draft.

Thank you,
John A. Student

Signing your name shows respect.

Says how long you need to meet.

Thanks the teacher.

Explains why you need to meet.

PUT YOUR KNOW-HOW TO WORK

Evaluate How You Communicate With Your Teacher
If you need to know something about an assignment from a teacher, practice using the rules on pages 51–52. **After your conversation, check how well you did the following:**

1. I talked to my teacher, even though I felt really shy:
__Yes
__No
__Not sure

2. I approached my teacher at a time when she wasn't busy:
__Yes
__No
__Not sure

3. I told my teacher directly what I wanted:
__Yes
__No
__Not sure

4. I looked my teacher in the eye:
__Yes
__No
__Not sure

5. I said please and thank you:
__Yes
__No
__Not sure

My goals for my next conversation with my teacher are:

_____.
(Write down the items above for which you checked "No" or "Not sure.")

This letter is directly addressed to the teacher, and it explains why the student wants to meet with her and how long the meeting will take. The student has done his part in preparing a draft for the teacher, rather than relying on the teacher to do everything. Finally, the student thanks the teacher for her time. The e-mail is not too casual in tone, and the spelling and grammar are correct.

UNDERSTANDING TEACHER EXPRESSIONS

Remember when your kindergarten teacher posted the rules in the classroom—rules like "keep your hands to yourself" and "raise your hand when you want to speak"? Things might have been a bit easier in kindergarten, when teachers made their rules very clear, or explicit. Teachers in middle school aren't always so clear. Instead, they expect you to be a fair and respectful participant in classroom discussions, and they don't expect to have to tell you exactly what to do.

Therefore, while teachers want you to understand them, you might not be very clear about what their expectations are, and the way they explain things might be confusing to you. It is your job as a student to listen to what teachers say, try to interpret what they mean, and then do what they say. If you don't understand, you must ask the teacher what he means.

Test yourself about the meaning of the following common teacher expressions. Do you understand what your teacher means when he says the following things?

plagiarism: Copying someone else's work, either intentionally by copying an article, wesbsite, book, or someone else's paper word for word or by forgetting to put what you read in your own words. Plagiarism is against the rules in school and can get you in trouble; your work is expected to be your own.

What your teacher says: "This work should be your own."
What your teacher means: Don't copy directly or word for word from the Internet or from another source like a book or a magazine. That is called **plagiarism**, and it's against the rules in school. Instead, paraphrase, or put the information into your own words. Cite or write down all your sources and give them to your teacher. Do not copy another person's work or let someone else do your work for you. In addition, do not let other kids copy your work.

What your teacher says: "Study chapters 5 and 6 (hint, hint)," or "Be sure to carefully look over chapters 5 and 6 this weekend."

What your teacher means: Your teacher is trying to tell you there

PUT YOUR KNOW-HOW TO WORK

Ask for Help Politely

Read the following students' emails to their teachers. Rate the emails as "well done," "pretty good," "okay," or "needs work." Use what you have learned in the previous example and use the rules at the end to decide how each student did.

Dear Ms. Smith:

I have a difficult time with spelling tests. I have tried to memorize spelling words by writing them each out, but I still do not do well on tests. I would like to meet with you to find ways I can do better. When would be a good time for me to meet with you? Thank you for your time.

Sophie

Hey teach,

Spelling is a waste of time. Everyone knows that. Computers fix seplling mistakes for you. I would like to meet with you to talk about this and about how to be let out of the requirement of taking spelling tests.

Sophie

Of these two students, which one:

__Addresses her teacher politely and by name?

__States exactly in which areas she needed help?

__Asks the teacher when would be a good time to meet?

__Thanks the teacher for her help?

__Treats the teacher and her subject respectfully?

next page

You might have guessed that the first student did a much better job of asking for help. She tells the teacher that she is trying to do better and has worked hard on her classwork but that she still can't do well. She asks the teacher when it would be convenient to meet to find out the teacher's suggestions about how to do better, and thanks the teacher for her time.

The second student is having the same problems as the first student, but most likely the way in which she asks for help will make the teacher feel reluctant to help her (though the teacher may do so, she will most likely be much more helpful to the first student, who is more polite). The second student does not show respect for the teacher's subject matter, and she asks to be let out of the requirement without showing the teacher that she is trying. In fact, this student even makes a spelling mistake in her e-mail, which isn't likely to make the teacher agree to help her. In addition, by making a spelling mistake, this student proves herself wrong, as she is using a computer and still made an error!

While both these students are having the same problem—doing poorly on spelling tests—and are both asking for the same thing—the teacher's help—the first student is much more likely to get help from the teacher than the second student.

Here's the lesson: *The way in which you ask for help is really important.* You should be polite, show that you are working hard, and ask the teacher for a convenient time to meet.

may be a surprise quiz or some kind of assignment on these chapters the following week, so you should study them before coming to class and prepare yourself by reading chapters 5 and 6.

What your teacher says: "Class participation is important."
What your teacher means: You should contribute relevant comments to each class discussion. "Relevant" means related to the subject you are studying, not to something you found interesting but that isn't closely related to the material in class. Don't **monopolize the conversation** or take over class discussion. You should also be

monopolize the conversation: Talk at length without letting others have a turn to speak.

respectful of your classmates. If they get the wrong answer or make a remark you consider silly or stupid, don't say anything and keep your opinion to yourself. Act engaged and don't show boredom in class.

What your teacher says: "Treat each other with respect."
What your teacher means: Don't insult your classmates or their ideas. If they are wrong, let the teacher correct them instead of correcting them yourself. If the teacher is wrong, don't correct him class. You could meet with him privately and mention the mistake in private (but first, check if the teacher actually made a mistake). Pointing out another person's mistakes in public only embarrasses and angers that person.

What your teacher says: "I want you to be honest with me and each other."
What your teacher means: The teacher means that it's all right for you to disagree with him or with your classmates on matters related to the school work or homework assignments. However, you can't be so honest that you hurt people's feelings. Do not tell your teachers or classmates that they are stupid or boring or ugly (even if you think that is true). In general, avoid words like "stupid," "ugly," "fat," and "boring," which are words that tend to make other people feel bad. Don't disagree with every point the teacher makes. Don't mention large disagreements in class. Instead, talk to your teacher in private if you'd like to speak further about something he said that you disagree with. However, it's all right to point out a small mistake, such as an arithmetic or spelling error, in class.

What your teacher says: "This is important," or "Write this down."
What your teacher means: This material may appear on the next test or quiz, and the teacher wants you to know it and be prepared by studying this information.

What your teacher says: "Neatness counts."
What your teacher means: Organize your work and write or type neatly, as the way your work looks will be part of your grade. If your work looks messy, your grade will be lower than if it were neatly written.

Teachers like students to participate in classroom discussions so that the students can learn by speaking and by hearing the remarks of their classmates. Classroom discussions are ways for people to talk about ideas and explain the material, and making mistakes is a natural part of the discussion.

Classmates are expected to allow each other to take turns during discussions so that everyone has roughly the same time to speak (though some people are more comfortable and more willing to voice their opinions than other people are).

Here are the basic rules for having a good classroom discussion. You are expected to:

➤ Contribute regularly to classroom discussions without taking them over or monopolizing the conversation. How do you know if you are monopolizing the conversation? It's all right for you to speak, but be sure to think about whether you are giving other kids a chance to speak too. If you have been speaking a lot during one class period, it's a good idea to give someone else a chance. If you've been speaking *for about one minute,* it may be time to give another kid or your teacher a chance to speak.

A lot of classroom discussion has to do with respecting other people's ideas, not just with the subject matter.

➤ Speak about the material you are currently studying and not about subjects that aren't related to the discussion.

➤ Praise a classmate for a good point with expressions such as, "What he said is interesting," or "I want to follow up on what she said."

➤ Follow up on what your classmate has just said by expanding on his or her point.

➤ Allow other people to speak.

➤ Allow for other kinds of opinions. It's all right if someone disagrees with you or comes up with another opinion, even if you think he is wrong. If you think there is factual evidence supporting your point, you can mention it, but then leave it alone. It's not your job to correct your classmates' errors—leave that to your teacher (who may sometimes not correct the other students).

➤ Check your body language: are you sitting up straight and looking your teacher and classmates in the eye?

Along with the rules for having a good classroom discussion, here are some things you should *avoid* doing because these things interfere with the discussion or are rude or disrespectful to your teachers or classmates:

➤ Interrupt your classmates or the teacher.

➤ Get the conversation off topic or just talk about your particular interest. This may be hard to do because you really want to talk about what interests you, whether it's a video game, a part of history, or music. Ask yourself whether what you want to say is related to the conversation going on in the classroom at that time.

➤ Disrespect the teacher or your classmates because they don't seem smart. Keep this type of opinion to yourself.

➤ Correct the teacher or your classmates, unless it's about a small factual error, such as a calculation mistake in math or a spelling mistake.

➤ Act bored by yawning or slumping in your chair.

➤ Be too shy to jump into the conversation at all.

Here is a conversation that might take place in your history class:

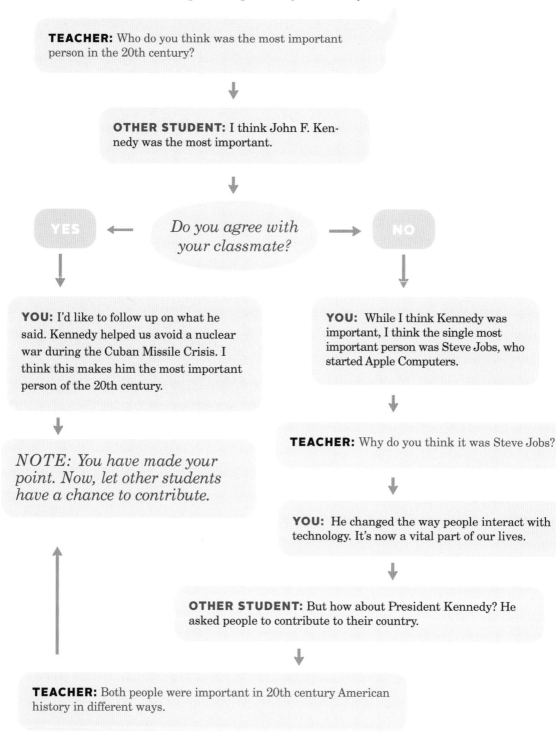

TEACHER: Who do you think was the most important person in the 20th century?

OTHER STUDENT: I think John F. Kennedy was the most important.

Do you agree with your classmate?

YES

NO

YOU: I'd like to follow up on what he said. Kennedy helped us avoid a nuclear war during the Cuban Missile Crisis. I think this makes him the most important person of the 20th century.

YOU: While I think Kennedy was important, I think the single most important person was Steve Jobs, who started Apple Computers.

NOTE: You have made your point. Now, let other students have a chance to contribute.

TEACHER: Why do you think it was Steve Jobs?

YOU: He changed the way people interact with technology. It's now a vital part of our lives.

OTHER STUDENT: But how about President Kennedy? He asked people to contribute to their country.

TEACHER: Both people were important in 20th century American history in different ways.

PUT YOUR KNOW-HOW TO WORK

Evaluate Your Participation in Class Discussions
It is your job to rate yourself. During a normal classroom discussion, note how often you do or do not do the following. Write "Never," "Sometimes" or "Every Day."

How often do you:

➤ Raise your hand to contribute? _____

➤ Connect your point to what a student has already said?
  _____

➤ Praise a fellow student for a good point?
  _____

➤ Have good body language, sitting up in the chair and looking others in the eye? _____

Good! Write here what you are doing well and need to continue:
_____

How often do you:

➤ Interrupt others? _____

➤ Go off on a point that was unrelated to the conversation?
  _____

➤ Put someone else down? _____

➤ Slouch in your chair or look down while talking?
  _____

Keep trying! Write down what you need to work on:
_____

GOAL SETTING:
CLASSROOM RULES

Now that you've read the rules of the classroom, write down some goals that you have. Make your goals SMART: that is, Specific, Measurable, Attainable, Realistic, and Timely. For example, here are some goals you might work towards:

➤ This semester, I will e-mail my history teacher to arrange extra-help sessions related to the research paper, a week before the paper is due.

➤ I will try to follow up on one comment by my classmates in my English class.

➤ I will work to make my body language better in class this semester by sitting up straight and looking my teacher in the eye.

In this chapter, you learned ways to treat your teacher and classmates respectfully and to follow the unwritten rules in the classroom. In the next chapter, you will learn some ways to handle other situations in school.

CHAPTER 5

OTHER SITUATIONS *in* SCHOOL

There are a lot of situations in school that take place outside of the classroom, such as recess and lunch, and there are some occasions when you follow a different routine, such as parties or concerts. While these are great times to relax and make friends, you may need strategies to help you interact with kids and understand situations that don't always have strict rules.

TEST YOURSELF:

How Well Do You Handle Recess, Lunch, and Other Situations in School?

1. During lunch, do you:
__a. try to eat in the classroom.
__b. eat by yourself in the cafeteria.
__c. eat with some friends you arranged to meet at a certain table.

2. When you have free time at school, do you:
__a. play video games by yourself.
__b. help your teacher clean the boards.
__c. participate in a club.

3. When there is a celebration or party, do you:
__a. sit at your desk.
__b. ask the teacher for a job to do during the party, such as passing out cups and plates.
__c. try to talk to the other kids.

4. When you are in gym class, do you:
__a. try to get out of playing sports.
__b. hang around the teachers.
__c. try to get into the game.

5. During recess, do you:
__a. try to stay inside in the classroom.
__b. shoot hoops or read by yourself.
__c. ask other kids if you can join the game they are playing.

If you answered mostly "a," you may need to read on in this chapter for some more ideas about how to reach out to people during social

> There are ways to make yourself more comfortable in the lunch room and at recess.

events at school. The other people at school, including the other kids and the teacher, may not realize what a great kid you are.

If you answered mostly "b," you are doing a great job establishing good relationships with the adults at your school. Use the strategies in this chapter to make friends with some other kids.

If you answered mostly "c," you are interacting with other kids and feel relatively comfortable during social events. In this chapter, find some other ways to make recess, lunch, and other occasions more enjoyable.

NAVIGATING RECESS, GYM, AND LUNCH

Here are some places at school where you might find yourself in a situation where you have to interact with a bunch of kids.

RECESS

Recess can be the best part of the day because you get to run around outside and burn off some steam. You can run free and play games without any teachers telling you it's time to practice your handwriting or take a spelling test. That's the good part.

Here's the bad part of recess. As you probably know, sometimes, kids act mean at recess. They make fun of other kids or try to hurt them. Be sure to report all **bullying** to your teacher. While not all behavior you don't like is bullying, if a kid tries to hurt you or if he says mean things about you, you should tell your teacher (or another responsible adult, such as your parents). You can tell the teacher what the other kids are doing in private so the other kids won't know about it. You can ask your teacher to talk to the other kid or you can ask the teacher for some tips about how to handle this situation on your own. See Chapter 7 for more ideas about how to handle bullies at school.

If you feel comfortable, you can join a game, such as four-square, tag, or kickball. You can ask to play in the game, or observe it for a while to find out what the rules are before you join in. It is best to wait your turn and not jump in the middle of a game. Wait for the next inning of kickball or the next round of four-square, then ask if you can join in.

GLOSSARY

bullying: aggressive behavior that is done on purpose to hurt someone. Bullying can take the form of physical or verbal abuse. In other words, bullies can try to hurt your body, or they can say mean things about you. Be sure to tell an adult if someone bullies you.

Here is an example of how you might ask to join in a game of four-square:

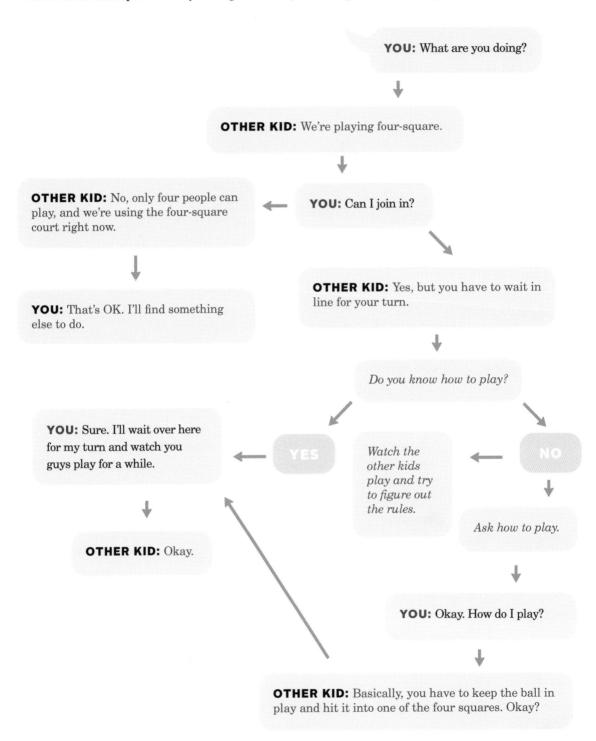

YOU: What are you doing?

OTHER KID: We're playing four-square.

OTHER KID: No, only four people can play, and we're using the four-square court right now.

YOU: Can I join in?

YOU: That's OK. I'll find something else to do.

OTHER KID: Yes, but you have to wait in line for your turn.

Do you know how to play?

YOU: Sure. I'll wait over here for my turn and watch you guys play for a while.

YES

Watch the other kids play and try to figure out the rules.

NO

Ask how to play.

OTHER KID: Okay.

YOU: Okay. How do I play?

OTHER KID: Basically, you have to keep the ball in play and hit it into one of the four squares. Okay?

If you don't want to join a game, you can join the conversation in the schoolyard instead. To join in the conversation, listen for a while or ask a friend, "what are you talking about?" Or you can also try to find kids in the playground doing something else, like playing in the garden (if there is one) or drawing. You can throw around a ball, or bring out a board game or cards to play with other kids. To find some other activities, look around the playground, or ask other kids what they do during recess.

If you can't find anyone else to play with, you can still stay outside and enjoy recess. You can try exercising or playing alone, shooting hoops, reading, or journaling. Your goal is to find the place that makes you feel the most comfortable and that allows you a few minutes of rest and relaxation during the school day.

GYM

Gym class can be hard if it's loud or a bit wild, and sometimes, it's hard to participate in the games. If there is a choice of games to play, you can ask your teacher to join the one that involves less physical contact, such as volleyball instead of wrestling. If you find that you have to participate in the game, try to ask a friend for help. For example, ask a friend to help you practice shooting baskets or kicking soccer balls around so that you can improve, if you feel that you need to get better in these areas. With a bit of practice, you may find that you can improve your game.

There are many ways to get physical activity that don't involve joining a team or loud noises, such as hiking or martial arts.

If gym continues to be a problem, you may have to ask your parents to speak to the teacher or the principal of your school. Ask the teacher for her ideas about how you can best join in the game in gym and whether another kid can help you. Though you may not always like gym, it is a good way to get to play with other kids. Physical exercise helps you feel less stressed, and it keeps you healthy.

Sometimes, there are other ways that your school will allow you to get credit for gym class, such as yoga, karate, or swimming, though not all schools offer these options. The important thing is to find an activity that you like to do. Exercise helps you stay in shape, and it also helps you feel less stressed. You may want to participate in these activities outside of school, in addition to taking gym class in school. There are many ways to get physical activity that don't involve being on a team or loud noises, such as:

➤ Dancing

➤ Hiking

➤ Yoga

➤ Martial arts, such as karate or tae kwon do

➤ Rock climbing

➤ Swimming

There are many other activities that make you feel better and allow you to keep in shape without necessarily playing on a team. Try to find the right activity for you.

These activities can be a great way to make friends, too, because you will be around people with whom you share a common interest and have something to talk about.

THE LUNCHROOM

At lunch, kids sit with other kids who are their friends. If you can find one or two buddies to eat with every day, it will help make lunch more comfortable. You may even agree to meet up with these kids in the lunchroom at a specific table. If you don't have lunch buddies, you can ask a nice kid if you can sit at her table. You can also join a group that meets during lunch, such as a club, to have something to do and people to eat with. If you can't find kids to eat with, ask your teacher if you can eat lunch in your classroom for a day. You don't want to eat lunch in the classroom every day, but it might be helpful just for one day if you are feeling stressed out. If you find somewhere to eat every day, you'll feel more comfortable at lunchtime. If you can't find somewhere to eat, find a trusted teacher, and ask that person for help. The teacher can suggest some kids you might sit with and help you figure out how to approach the kids.

At lunch, kids like to talk about sports, music, movies, and what they did or are doing over the weekend. One good way to jump into the conversation is to ask someone if she saw a movie that you did or if she watches the same television shows. You can also ask other kids what they are going to do this weekend. Teachers are a favorite topic of conversation, though you don't want to speak negatively about a teacher or another kid. Other things to talk about might be: hobbies and collectibles (like Pokémon cards), popular cartoon or comic book characters, inventions, or hypothetical questions like "would you rather have superhuman strength or be able to fly?"

One problem you may run into is that kids who've been sitting together for a while like to have **inside jokes** that only they understand. If you encounter this situation, don't panic. Just smile, and eventually, you will get the joke—or at least know when to laugh. If the kids are making fun of another kid, you may want to change the subject. You don't want to make laughing at other kids the basis of your conversation, and, if this behavior persists, you might want to find a different group of kids.

It's okay if you don't feel like talking to other people or prefer to eat by yourself. Recognize that if other kids try to talk to you, they are only being friendly—most of the time—and they aren't trying to interrupt you or disturb you.

DEALING WITH SPECIAL OCCASIONS AT SCHOOL

There are some times when you may be asked to participate in other activities at school, such as a birthday party, a graduation, or a concert. Here are some tips about how to behave in these types of situations.

BIRTHDAY PARTIES

You've probably been to birthday parties at kids' houses. Birthday celebrations at school are similar. They can be loud and annoying, but a lot of kids like them. You are expected to sing happy birthday (if it's too loud, do your best to get through it or excuse yourself to go to the bathroom) and to wish the birthday boy or girl a happy birthday. One good part is that the kids usually bring snacks like cupcakes to school.

On your birthday, you may choose not to have a school celebration, and that's fine. You can simply tell the teacher ahead of time that you

inside joke: A joke that is funny only to the people that know the situation behind it. In other words, you have to know the joke beforehand to find it funny. It is also sometimes called an "in-joke."

find these types of parties loud and irritating. However, if you would like a party, go ahead and have one. After you get through the singing, you can have cake or cupcakes, if your teacher allows that in the classroom.

GRADUATIONS

Often, teachers have celebrations on the last day of school. They may ask you to step up to the front of the classroom and get a diploma, or a piece of paper that says you can move up to the next grade. Parents and friends may be invited, and the kids in your class may sing or make speeches. You are expected to stay quiet when other kids are talking, and to step forward when the teacher calls you.

If you feel worried about these types of events, ask the teachers ahead of time what to expect. That way, you won't be surprised on the day of the celebration, and you can think of ways to get through the tough parts, such as the singing or the stepping forward to the front of the class. Once you've been to this type of celebration, future similar events will be easier, because you will know what to expect. If you ask your teacher for advance notice about changes in routine, it will help you navigate special events like graduations and birthday parties.

CONCERTS

Often, middle schools have concerts or assemblies on holidays, such as on Thanksgiving, or during the winter holidays. Usually, kids play instruments and sing, or they may act in plays. The teachers or principal may also speak to the students. While you may not want to participate directly or be required to do so (unless you want to, of course), you are expected to clap at the end of each performance, even if you think it's bad, and to stay silent during the concert. If you think the noise will bother you, you can speak to your teacher in advance about sitting in the back of the room.

PUT YOUR KNOW-HOW TO WORK

Think About How You Manage Difficult Situations at School
What would you do in the following situations?

1. You look around the lunch room, but you don't know anyone.

a. You sit down by yourself and hope someone will join you.
b. You ask to sit with someone you recognize from your math class.
c. You plan to meet up with some friends the next day.

Any of these ideas might work. It's good to make a plan to sit with some friends the next day so you won't find yourself in the same situation.

2. You don't have anything to do during recess.

a. You ask to join in a game of tag that some other kids are playing.
b. You bring out a board game and ask some other kids if they want to play.
c. You find a shady spot and read by yourself.

All of these are good ways to spend recess, and you may even enjoy it!

3. You don't like the loud kickball game going on in gym class.

a. You ask to sit on the sidelines and not play.
b. You pretend you are sick and go to the nurse's office.
c. You plan to be absent next week when you have gym.

These aren't the best ways to handle this situation; can you think of any others?

SUBSTITUTE TEACHERS

Sometimes, your teachers are unexpectedly absent from school, usually because they are temporarily sick or because they have to attend
a meeting somewhere else. In this case, you will have a substitute
teacher, and this person won't know you. It can be very difficult to
have another teacher for the day, and the unexpected situation can
make you feel nervous and unsure. Here are some ways you might
handle this situation:

➤➤ Ask your teacher to leave a note for a substitute teacher in case
the teacher is absent; the note might state that you may act a
bit nervous or anxious with another teacher in the room but that
you are doing your best to get along with the teacher.

➤➤ Remember that the substitute teacher is new, too. How do you
think she is feeling? Do you think it's possible that the sub feels
nervous too?

➤➤ To make yourself (and the sub) feel better, you may want to offer
to help the sub with the names of people in the class or the loca-
tion of the classroom supplies.

➤➤ After you've had some substitute teachers, you may realize that
while the situation isn't as comfortable as having your regular
teacher, you can get through the day or a class with a sub.

It may help to remember that if the sub acts mean, it is probably just because she is trying hard and is worried about keeping control of the class.

Try to help the sub during a break, not in the middle of classroom discussion.

FINDING OTHER WAYS TO MAKE FRIENDS WITH KIDS AND ADULTS AT SCHOOL

There are other situations outside the classroom that you don't have
to participate in, but that might offer opportunities to make friends
with other kids or adults. Consider whether some of the situations
below describe social opportunities that you'd like to become involved
with:

➤➤ Helping younger kids. You may be very patient with younger
kids and enjoy being around them. They are usually very happy
to be around older kids and easy to teach. Ask your teacher

about chances to visit other classrooms to teach the younger kids math or to read them stories.

➤➤ Helping other kids with computers or another area of interest. Your teacher can help you come up with ways to join in the classroom by teaching the class about your skill or interest—whether it's chess, computers, or history.

➤➤ Working in the library. Librarians are a great connection for you in your school. They can direct you to books in your area of interest and maybe let you hang out and relax in a quiet, peaceful place. They may also let you read to other kids or use their computers.

➤➤ Talking to adults. There are a lot of adults in your school you may not have thought of befriending, such as the people who work in the lunch room or computer lab or who keep the school clean. These types of adults are often interesting to speak with and can be friends who make school a more welcoming place.

GOAL SETTING:
RULES FOR OTHER SITUATIONS IN SCHOOL

Now that you've read the rules of classroom, write down some goals that you have. Make your goals SMART: that is, Specific, Measurable, Attainable, Realistic, and Timely. For example, here are some goals you might work towards:

➤➤ I will attend the weekly Spanish club meeting during lunchtime this week.

➤➤ During recess, I will ask to join in the basketball game once this week.

➤➤ I will ask my teacher what to expect at the upcoming school concert, and arrange to sit in the back, if possible.

In this chapter, you learned some strategies for handling situations that generally take place outside of the classroom at school. Next, you will learn some ways to connect with other kids at school and outside of school.

CHAPTER 6

FRIENDS, CLASSMATES, *and the* OTHER KIDS

You spend a lot of time at school with your classmates, and you may find them annoying and frustrating at times. It may seem strange to you when kids do things like:

➤ shout for no reason

➤ spend time talking about nothing

➤ imitate each other

➤ make fun of each other for no reason

It may seem at times like the other kids are speaking a totally different language—one that makes no sense whatsoever—but there are ways to find friends in this confusing situation. This chapter will help you understand the other kids and how to make friends in school.

TEST YOURSELF: How Do You Interact With the Other Kids at School?

1. When you want to start a conversation with someone, do you:
__a. Say nothing and expect the other person to start talking.
__b. Start talking about something that interests you.
__c. Ask the person what he is doing.

2. When you are at recess, do you:
__a. Play by yourself.
__b. Watch other kids play.
__c. Try to join in the game.

3. Do you join clubs at school?
__a. No, I don't like clubs.
__b. I'm not sure what clubs there are to join.
__c. I join clubs, such as drama or robotics, with people who share my interests.

4. When other kids laugh at a joke, do you:
__a. Ignore them because you don't understand why they are laughing.

__b. Laugh nervously.

__c. Ask someone to explain the joke to you.

5. When you want to play with kids outside of school, do you:

__a. Hope they ask you to their house.

__b. Try to sit at their lunch table.

__c. Invite kids over to your house.

If you answered mostly "a," you are a great kid, but the other kids at your school may not always know about you or your interests. You may need the help of a friendly teacher to make friends with other kids who share your interests. Read on in this chapter to find ways to start finding friends and understanding kids at school.

If you answered mostly "b," you interact with some kids like you, and that's great. It's okay to spend time with one or two special friends. After all, quality matters more than quantity when it comes to friends. Read on in this chapter to start to figure out how to get to know other kids in your school.

social butterfly: a person who has a lot of friends and talks a lot.

If you answered mostly "c," you sound like a **social butterfly**. You clearly feel comfortable with kids at your school and know how to interact with them. Read on to discover how you might start making friends with other kids and to figure out how well you treat other kids and how well they treat you.

MAKING FRIENDS

You can join a club to find kids who share your interests—whether it's computers, robotics, chess, or drama, there are other kids out there who like the same thing.

You have a great personality and lots of interests, so you may wonder why it's sometimes hard to make friends. Part of it is because other kids may not know you very well. Sometimes, it's just a matter of finding the right group of kids who appreciate you and learning how to talk to them. Here are some ways you can get to know kids who you'd like to hang out with:

➤ Try to find kids who share your interests. You'll find you have more in common with them.

➤ Look for clubs to join that have kids with your interests or skills.

➤ Learn the scripts, or patterns, of common conversations so you can participate in them more easily.

➤ Learn easy ways to have fun with kids that don't always involve conversation, such as video or board games, sports games (especially just throwing around a ball or doing something noncompetitive), or watching movies.

➤ Understand what people are saying with their bodies, not just their words.

➤ Understand that sometimes, kids just fool around for no reason.

➤ Know that kids sometimes say silly things just to amuse themselves. There may be little meaning to what they say, but they might just think it's funny, even if it doesn't seem particularly funny to you.

Just as there are things to do, here are a few things to consider not doing:

➤ Don't hang out with kids who bully you. If you are physically threatened, or hit, or if you are teased and insulted, report this to your teacher or another trusted adult right away.

➤ Don't hang out with other kids who do things that make you uncomfortable. This may include teasing another kid, hurting someone else, or saying mean things about your teacher.

➤ Don't force yourself to be sociable all the time if you don't feel like it.

➤ Don't allow other kids to do anything that makes you feel uncomfortable, emotionally or physically.

➤ Don't make fun of kids who are different than you.

➤ Don't be overly negative about yourself and don't believe what mean kids say about you. If someone says something hurtful about you, try your best to ignore what was said. The kid who said it was just trying to upset you or be mean to you.

Remembering what the other kid likes shows that you are interested in talking to him.

When you are interacting with another kid, you want to remember a bit about him and about your previous interactions. In a way, it's like making the transition from math class to English class. In math class, you speak in symbols, while in English class, the conversation is different. If you are trying to play with or start a conversation with another kid, ask yourself:

➤ What do I remember about this kid from my previous conversations? Is there a specific interest he has, or something that he likes to talk about? In addition, are there things he doesn't like to talk about or things that bother him?

➤ What kinds of things did I do with this kid in the past, and would she be interested in doing the same thing again?

You might discover that you share some of the same interests.

➤ Is this kid usually nice or mean to me? If he is mean, can I try to avoid him or talk to someone else? If he is nice, can I find ways to find out more about him?

➤ Have I ever been involved in an activity or class with this kid before? If so, can I speak to her about it?

You could start keeping a journal to record information about the other kids and what they like.

Remembering what you know about each kid can help you speak to him and build a relationship. Try to keep a record of what interests some of the kids you would like to be better friends with, so you can speak to them and develop friendships with them.

HAVING CONVERSATIONS

Conversations between kids at school tend to follow some general scripts, though not always. That means that some basic conversations are like recipes for making food or like formulas in science. They tend to follow the same route and include the same parts, or ingredients.

Some common types of conversation include the following:

➤ Someone asking you what you did over the weekend. In this case, you can just tell the other person what you did and ask her what she did.

➤ Someone asking you if you saw a movie or television show. In this case, you can tell the other person if you did or didn't. If you did, you can tell him what you thought of the show. If you didn't, you can ask him what it was about.

➤ Someone asking you about a teacher or the homework. You can just tell the person the factual information about the class.

There are some scripts you can follow when talking to other people. Conversations tend to take similar paths, and you can find a way to participate in them.

➤ Someone talking about another friend. This is often a gossipy kind of conversation, and you can feel free not to participate in it by simply saying you don't really know much about the other person and excusing yourself.

➤ Someone talking about a shared hobby or interest. It's great to be part of a club because you can easily have a conversation about what you are doing as part of that club—whether it's the Scouts or robotics. Talking about a common interest makes it easier to start a conversation and keep it going.

➤ Sometimes, conversations are really about nothing. Kids just like to say silly things or kid around. It's okay for them to talk nonsense—that's just their idea of fun, whether or not it might be your idea. You can just listen and wait for a chance to ask a question.

Here's an example of a type of conversation you might have at lunch:

CLASSMATE: Me and my dad are going to see the new movie on African cats this weekend. *(This opening sentence means that you should comment on the movie.)*

↓

Have you seen the movie?

YES ← → NO

↓

YOU: That's cool. I saw that last weekend.

YOU: I don't know about that movie. Can you tell me more about it?

↓

CLASSMATE: What did you think about it?

↓

YOU: It's a great movie. Lots of gory hunting scenes. *(Here, give your opinion, but don't give away the ending. For example, don't say, "You will hate the ending because the main character dies." People like to be surprised when they see the ending of movies.)* → **CLASSMATE:** I love gory scenes, especially when there's like blood dripping down the cats.

↓ ↓

Follow up on what your class-mate says.

Or move on to another topic.

↓ ↓

YOU: There is a lot of blood in this movie.

YOU: What other kinds of movies do you like?

USEFUL CONVERSATION STARTERS

Sometimes, it's just hard to know what to talk about in lunch or at other times. Here are some topics you can bring up to start a conversation:

➤ What are you doing this weekend?

➤ Do you know what the homework is?

➤ Did you watch the game last night?

➤ Did you watch *American Idol* last night?

➤ Do you play Angry Birds? What is your highest score? How do you play?

➤ Are you interested in singing or dancing?

➤ Are you interested in making things with Legos?

This is also a good way to start a conversation on the phone with other kids.

Talk about a sporting event or your favorite teams.

Discuss a popular TV show.

Talk about a video game that you like to play.

Discuss an activity that you enjoy.

Ask the other kid if he shares an interest that you have.

When someone answers your question, either follow up with what you like, or contribute a follow-up question.

And remember, everyone loves it when you ask his or her opinion. That's right—the easiest way to start a really long conversation is to ask another kid, "What did you think of that class?" or "What do you think about that TV show or book?" Just listen to the answer, and you've started a good conversation!

MOVE ON IN CONVERSATION

Sometimes, even if you are interested in a topic, the other person will indicate that he wants to talk about something else by bringing up a new subject. If this happens, you can mention one more thing about your subject by saying, "Oh, just one more thing...." But then it's time to move on to another subject. If you persist in talking about something when the other person is ready to move on, you may appear rude (though you don't mean to be), or the person you are speaking to may get bored.

Here are some signs that the other person is ready to move on to talk about something else:

➤ The other person brings up another topic.

➤ The other person yawns, taps her foot, or looks at her watch.

➤ The person looks away.

If you look carefully, you may notice that the person is giving you these signs and is ready to talk about a new topic.

COMMON EXPRESSIONS

A lot of expressions that people use don't really mean what they appear to mean. Here are some examples of phrases—and there are many others—that you shouldn't interpret literally. That means, the words mean something else than what they appear to mean. If you want to know more **idioms**, which are terms that don't literally mean what they say, check out *Scholastic Dictionary of Idioms* by Marvin Terban.

idioms: expressions such as "raining cats and dogs" that don't mean exactly what they say.

What a person says: "You don't even know."
What a person means: This doesn't mean that you don't know what you are talking about. Instead, it means that what you said is only the beginning and that there's even more to what you are saying. In other words, this expression means that you are right.
What a person says: "You wouldn't believe it!"
What a person means: This doesn't actually mean that you would not believe what the person is saying. They are describing something surprising or unusual, and exaggerating for dramatic effect.
What a person says: "Forget about it!"
What a person means: This does not actually mean that you should forget something. It is just an expression meaning, "wow!"

Here are some other expressions that don't mean exactly what they say:

➤ "hot water": If someone is in "hot water," it means she is in trouble, not literally in a vat of hot water.

PUT YOUR KNOW-HOW TO WORK

Practice Conversations

How should you answer the following statements in conversation?

Pick the best answer.

1. CLASSMATE: What did you do this weekend?

How should you answer?

__a. I really like Legos.
__b. Have you played Super Mario Galaxy?
__c. I played video games with my brother. How about you?

2. CLASSMATE: What did you think of that test we just took?

How should you answer?

__a. Not much.
__b. I thought it was easy.
__c. It was all right. What did you think?

3. CLASSMATE: Do you want to hang out this weekend?

How should you answer?

__a. No.
__b. I think I'm busy.
__c. I'd like to. Let me just check with my mom and get back to you, okay?

4. CLASSMATE: Do you know what the homework is?

How should you answer?

next page

__a. No idea.

__b. I'm not sure.

__c. I don't know, but let me check my planner and let you know.

The best answers are "c" in the examples above. While all the answers may be factually correct—you may not know what the homework is and, in fact, you may not want to hang out with your classmate over the weekend—it's a good idea not to hurt other people's feelings with answers that are too direct. Notice that the answer choice "c" responds directly to your classmate's question rather than going off on a tangent or an unrelated topic. The correct answer also often includes a way to ask the classmate his or her opinion on the subject.

➡ "the ropes": If someone has to learn "the ropes," that means he has to learn how to do things. There are no ropes actually involved.

➡ "it goes on forever": This means that something just goes on for a long time, not literally forever.

BODY LANGUAGE

While having a conversation, you should try to look the other person in the eye, at least some of the time. Here's what your friend may be trying to tell you with her body language (though each person uses body language differently, so what people are trying to say with these behaviors may change, depending on the person and the conversation):

> People's body language can give you clues about how they are feeling.

➡ **Looking at her watch or the clock:** This means your friend is eager to end the conversation and has to go somewhere else.

➡ **Tapping her foot:** Again, this is a sign that your friend needs to end the conversation and may be bored or impatient.

➡ **Crossing her arms:** This may mean your friend is upset about what you are saying or feels hurt or defensive.

PUT YOUR KNOW-HOW TO WORK

Identify Expressions

Using your skills of observation, you can listen carefully in conversations and develop a list of expressions that don't mean what they actually say. There are four idioms bolded in the following passage. Try to figure out what they mean, or look at the definitions below to help you.

The school drama production was a **blessing in disguise** for Sophie. At first, she was worried about it, and she thought that in trying out for the play, she was **barking up the wrong tree.** She was even scared to ask her teacher to try out, and she **beat around the bush** for a while when talking to her teacher. However, the audience simply went **head over heels** over her performance, and she felt very good about it.

Blessing in disguise: A hidden opportunity
Barking up the wrong tree: Doing the wrong thing
Beat around the bush: Did not get to the point
Head over heels: Very enthusiastic

➤ **Looking down at the floor:** This may be a sign that your friend is upset.

➤ **Raising her eyebrows:** This may show that the other person is surprised or doesn't believe what she is hearing.

➤ **Looking away:** This may show that the person is ready to end the conversation or is distracted by something else.

➤ **Making her voice louder:** This may mean the other person is getting angry or upset.

➤ **Making her voice quieter:** This may mean that the person is scared or upset.

PUT YOUR KNOW-HOW TO WORK

Guess How Other Kids Are Feeling
Can you guess what the kids in these situations are feeling?

1. You are talking about your new video game and your high score. Your friend has been listening for a few minutes, but now, she looks away and tries to get someone else's attention.

_____.

(Notice that your friend might be a bit bored, if she is looking away and trying to talk to someone else. To get her interested in the conversation again, you might ask her something about herself, such as "Which games do you play?")

2. You are speaking to your friend about your favorite movie. He leans in and responds "yeah" many times. Then he starts talking about his opinion about this movie, which he also liked.

_____.

(Notice that this friend is really interested in the conversation because he is leaning in and participating and adding his own experience to what you've already said. You can keep talking about this movie.)

3. A boy in your class asks you what you think of his drawing. He shows it to you, and you say, "Well, what is it? I can't even tell. It's not very good."

_____.

(This boy's feelings may be hurt by what you told him. A lot of people enjoy doing things even if they aren't very good at them. Even if a kid's work isn't good, he will feel hurt if you say his work is bad. Instead, you may just want to nod and ask what he drew. Again, you can always ask him what he thinks of the picture, and listen to his response. You will have started a conversation.)

DEALING WITH ANNOYING SITUATIONS

Sometimes, you will feel annoyed at other kids. It's normal to feel irritated, but you should ask yourself whether the other kid tried to annoy you or did so **unintentionally**. For example, some kids like to yell or make a lot of noise. While you may find this really irritating, being noisy may be the other kid's idea of how to have fun. Here are some questions to ask yourself if another kid is annoying you:

unintentionally: by accident

▶ Does this person really mean to irritate me?

▶ Has this person tried to annoy me in the past?

▶ Does this person usually do nice things for me and act politely towards me?

▶ Is anyone else annoyed by this person's behavior? Has the teacher asked him to stop?

▶ Is there a reason this person is acting irritating—for example, we just had a hard test, or we're tired? In other words, could this kid just be upset, and that's why he is acting mean or wild?

If you are annoyed, what's the best way to handle the situation? Here are some options:

▶ Leave your friend and return when you are in a better mood.

▶ Tell this person in a polite way to stop doing what's irritating you—whether it's yelling, drawing on your paper, or something else.

▶ Start playing with something else or put on headphones, if you aren't in class.

Here are some things that aren't good choices:

▶ Yelling at another kid.

➤	Insulting the other person.

➤	Calling him names.

If the other kid acts annoying to you on a lot of occasions, he or she may be trying to bully you. See Chapter 7 for more information about how to handle this type of situation.

SAYING "NO"

It can be difficult to say no to a persuasive person, particularly if you would like that person to be your friend. *But you are not obligated, or required, to say yes to things, people, or situations that make you feel uncomfortable.* True friends do not make you do any of the following things:

➤	Lie about something.

➤	Cheat.

➤	Give them money, except a little bit in an emergency.

➤	Make you do their work or cheat off you.

➤	Make you do anything uncomfortable physically.

➤	Make you end a friendship with another person.

If someone asks you to do something that is uncomfortable, you have to say no clearly and calmly. Here are some strategies for saying no:

➤	State that you don't want to do what the person has asked you.

➤	Stay calm. Try not to get upset, if you can avoid it. If you get upset, you may not be able to handle the situation as effectively.

➤	If the other person asks why, you can just say that you feel uncomfortable.

➼ If the person will not take no for an answer, you can walk away.

➼ If the person is insistent and won't give up, talk to an adult you trust. The adult may be able to provide you with some ideas about how to talk to the other person, or the adult may have to step into the situation.

Remember, you have the right to say no to anything that makes you uncomfortable. Real friends will not push you to go along with something you don't want to do.

PUT YOUR KNOW-HOW TO WORK

Practice Saying No
Practice saying no in the following situations. You can do a role-play with a friend or adult.

1. Another kid in your class asks to copy your homework. Say no to him in a way that is calm but clear. If he persists, practice walking away.

2. Another kid in your grade keeps putting her arms around you, even though you've told her not to touch you. Practice telling her that this is not okay. If she doesn't listen, practice saying no again and walking away.

3. A friend asks you to borrow money. Tell him no and explain that you are willing to help him in another way. For example, you can share food if he's hungry. Explain that your parents do not allow you to lend money to people, except small amounts in emergencies.

APOLOGIZING TO KIDS

Even the wisest person makes mistakes. It's completely human, and there will come a time when you have made a mistake related to a friend or another kid and will have to apologize. For example, you may forget someone's birthday or leave them out of a get together.

If you make a mistake and need to apologize, here's the best way to do it:

➤ Speak clearly and say that you are sorry to your friend in person. Usually, e-mail and texts don't mean as much as speaking to someone face-to-face, and the other person will think you are more sincere if you speak to him face-to-face.

➤ Don't make excuses for your behavior. Your friend won't want to hear them and won't think you are truly sorry if you make excuses for what you did.

➤ State what you will do to make things up to your friend. For example, if you forget her birthday, you can tell her that you will invite her over for a late birthday celebration. Sometimes, just saying you're sorry is enough.

good faith attempt:
Making an effort and trying really hard, even if you do not get the outcome you wanted.

➤ If your friend doesn't forgive you and you have made a **good faith attempt** to apologize, you may have to accept that he needs some time to think about the situation. The best thing to do is to back off and try to find another situation in a few days to do something nice for your friend or to speak to him again.

JOINING AN ACTIVITY

If you are in the classroom or part of a club, you may need to join an activity that has already started with a group of kids. Joining an activity that is already going on is like tuning in late to your favorite television show. You may not know what is going on for the first few minutes. However, if you listen and watch, you will have a better idea of what's going on and how to jump into the action.

If kids are already playing in the playground or doing an activity in the classroom, you may want to watch for a few minutes before jumping in. You can also ask questions like, "What's going on?" or "How do I play?" Be sure that you understand the rules of the game or activity before jumping in. If you find it hard to get involved, you can say something like, "Can I join you?" or "Do you need help?"

ARRANGING A GET TOGETHER

If you want to hang out with another kid outside of school, you can ask him over. If you can't do so in person, you can always e-mail or text the other kid if you find that easier. Try to arrange your own get-togethers without asking your parents to do so. If you need help planning how to ask another kid over, you can ask your parents for help. Work with your parents to come up with some ideas of what to say to the other kid, but make the call yourself. The other kid might think you are acting really young if you have your parents call him. A great way to arrange a get together is to call up a kid after school to ask about the homework. That gives you something to talk about before you bring up hanging out.

You can also think about something that you might have in common with the other kid. For example, do you both like to play video games? If so, you can invite the other kid over to play games and explain which ones you have. If you are in a club with another kid, you can invite her over to practice whatever it is you do in that club—such as sports, drama, or building with Legos.

Try to make a plan ahead of time so you have some activities you can do with the other kid you invite over. For example, you can do activities such as:

➤ building things with Legos

➤ playing a board game or word game

➤ shooting baskets

➤ playing video games

➤ watching a movie

➤ cooking something, with your parents' supervision

PRACTICE ASKING A KID OVER

Fill in the blanks in the conversation below. This guide might help you ask another kid over to your house. You can use this type of script, or rehearsed speech, in person or on the phone.

You don't have to follow this script exactly. It just gives you some ideas that you might use in your conversation.

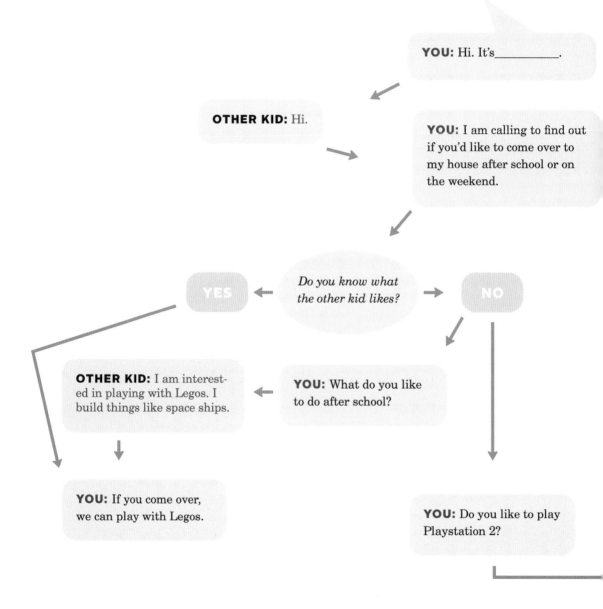

YOU: Hi. It's_____.

OTHER KID: Hi.

YOU: I am calling to find out if you'd like to come over to my house after school or on the weekend.

Do you know what the other kid likes?

YES   NO

OTHER KID: I am interested in playing with Legos. I build things like space ships.

YOU: What do you like to do after school?

YOU: If you come over, we can play with Legos.

YOU: Do you like to play Playstation 2?

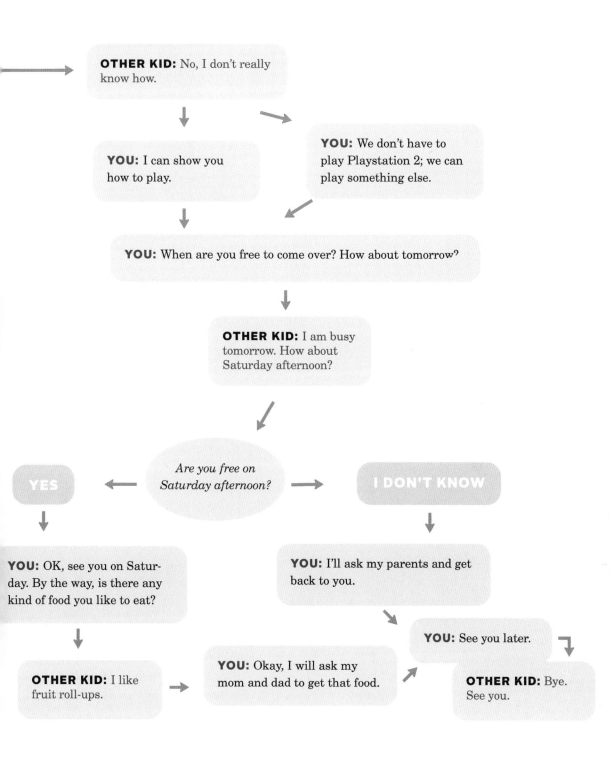

OTHER KID: No, I don't really know how.

YOU: I can show you how to play.

YOU: We don't have to play Playstation 2; we can play something else.

YOU: When are you free to come over? How about tomorrow?

OTHER KID: I am busy tomorrow. How about Saturday afternoon?

Are you free on Saturday afternoon?

YES

I DON'T KNOW

YOU: OK, see you on Saturday. By the way, is there any kind of food you like to eat?

YOU: I'll ask my parents and get back to you.

YOU: See you later.

OTHER KID: I like fruit roll-ups.

YOU: Okay, I will ask my mom and dad to get that food.

OTHER KID: Bye. See you.

If the conversation doesn't go as well as you had wanted, and the person is busy, try finding time to spend with that person at school. You may want to ask him over one more time before giving up. If it just doesn't work out with that kid, don't give up. Try to find another kid, especially through an activity you have in common, to invite over.

KNOWING THE RULES FOR HANGING OUT WITH OTHER KIDS

When a kid comes over to your house, you have an important role to play as a host. You have to make the other kid feel comfortable, and you need to be sure you are doing things the other kid enjoys. Here are some rules for being a good host:

➤ Start by asking the other kid what she would like to do. If she doesn't want to do something you want to, you may have to do what she wants for a little while. Remember, your guest gets the first choice of what to do.

➤ Offer your guest your stuff and your food.

➤ If there are games or other things you don't want the other kid to see, put them away before he arrives.

➤ Tell your guest ahead of time what time he should go home or call his parents, so you both know how long the get-together will be beforehand.

If you find that you don't have a lot in common with other kids in your school or aren't comfortable arranging times to hang out, look for clubs to join in your neighborhood, such as the Boy Scouts or Girl Scouts, or classes or sports at the local YMCA. These clubs will allow you to hang out with other kids who share your interests. There are lots of other clubs, too. Ask your parents to find you a place, either in your neighborhood or at school, where kids share your interest, whether it's karate, robotics, drama, chess, or history.

BEING A GOOD FRIEND

Being a good friend means that you treat other people in the way you would like to be treated. Don't make friends feel uncomfortable in any way or ask them to do things you wouldn't want to do. When thinking about how to treat other people, always ask yourself how you would feel in that situation. If you would feel uncomfortable in a situation, you shouldn't put other people in that same situation.

WHAT ARE SOME THINGS YOU SHOULD NEVER SAY IN PUBLIC?

Sometimes, people may mistakenly think you are bullying or insulting them by saying the wrong things in public. You may hurt other people's feelings without meaning to. Here are some things you should not say about people in public:

➤➤ You are fat.

➤➤ You are ugly.

➤➤ You are stupid.

➤➤ You smell bad.

➤➤ I don't like people who look like you.

➤➤ I don't like the color of your skin.

➤➤ I don't like bald people

➤➤ Why are you bald?

➤➤ I don't like glasses or crutches or wheelchairs.

➤➤ I don't like girls.

➤➤ I don't like boys.

➤➤ I don't like old people.

➤   I don't like people with accents.

➤   Why don't you speak English well?

The statements above could hurt people's feelings because they can't help being the way they are. Can you think of other things that you should not say in public because you might hurt people's feelings?

_____

_____

_____

_____

_____

_____

GOAL SETTING:
FRIENDS AND CLASSMATES RULES

Now that you've read the rules about dealing with other kids, write down some goals that you have. Make your goals SMART: that is, Specific, Measurable, Attainable, Realistic, and Timely. For example, here are some goals you might work towards:

➤   This week, I will try to find out about clubs in my school that I might get involved with. I will talk to my teacher about joining a robotics club.

➤   I will try to follow up on two comments by people at lunch today.

➤   When someone changes the subject, I will try to move on and talk about what that person is talking about.

In this chapter, you learned ways to start becoming better friends with kids at school. In the next chapter, you will learn how to avoid and deal with bullies or with kids who aren't good friends.

CHAPTER 7

BULLIES
and
MEAN KIDS

Bullying can be a serious issue in schools. Bullying means that another kid is doing something to harm you, either by saying mean things about you or by harming you physically. If you are in doubt about whether a kid is bullying you, be sure to report the kid's behavior to a teacher or a parent. Keep in mind that another kid should never touch you, except on the shoulder or the hand, and if a kid touches you somewhere else (except in sports), tell an adult. Also keep in mind that annoying behavior isn't always bullying; just because a kid is acting loud or wild, he may not be bullying you. Again, if you are in doubt, ask an adult you trust.

TEST YOURSELF: How Well Do You Handle Bullies?

1. If someone asks you to make a bet for money, do you:
__a. Politely say no.
__b. Ask him why he wants to make a bet.
__c. Hand over the money, if you have it.

2. When your classmate sends you a mean text message, do you:
__a. Not respond but show it to your teacher.
__b. Respond to the text in a mean way.
__c. Not respond to it or show it to anyone.

3. If other people are gathered around a mean or nasty picture of a classmate on a cell phone or computer, do you:
__a. Walk away and tell a teacher or another adult about the picture.
__b. Look at the picture but do nothing.
__c. Ask the classmate to e-mail you a copy of the picture.

4. If someone asks to copy off your homework or test, do you:
__a. Politely refuse and tell an adult.
__b. Just walk away.
__c. Give the person your homework.

5. If your classmate continually insults or makes fun of you, do you:
__a. Calmly and politely tell the person to stop, and tell a teacher if the insults continue.

__b. Ignore the insults.

__c. Lash out at the person and insult him or her back.

If you answered mostly "a," you are doing a great job dealing with bullies. In general, the correct way to respond to bullying is to *ask the person to stop in a calm way*. Do not respond by lashing out at the person, and, if the person doesn't stop, you need to report his behavior to a teacher or a trusted adult privately, without the other kids around. Remember, bullying other kids in school is usually against the law, and it's always wrong. Read on to find more information on how to handle bullies.

If you answered mostly "b," you are not engaging in bullying yourself, but you may be trying to ignore bad behavior and lies from your classmates or other people without doing anything about it. If you don't ask a bully to stop or report his behavior, you may not be able to stop his mean actions towards you or another person. Don't be afraid to ask for help—from a friend, a teacher, a parent, or another adult—if you feel that you can't handle bullies on your own.

If you answered mostly "c," you may be following bullies' leads and copying them. Remember that if you join in bullying or making fun of others, you are just as guilty as they are. There are rules against bullying other kids in school, and don't try to protect yourself by turning against other kids. Remember that you could be the next target of a bully, and report any bullying to a teacher.

DEALING WITH BULLIES

Some bullies are easy to spot. They try to boss around other kids, and they threaten kids with physical harm if they don't do what they want. Sometimes the bully may be the biggest kid in the class, or he may just have a loud mouth. He likes to boss people around and may sometimes tell kids he is going to hurt them. There are some strategies to deal with these kinds of bullies. You may want to try the following:

➡️ **Try to avoid them, without appearing scared.** Travel with a friend in the hallways and at recess, if possible. Don't run away from bullies, but try to avoid them, if possible. If you travel in a pair or group, bullies will be less likely to bother you.

➽ **Act confident.** Look the bully in the eye, and tell her you are not afraid. Usually, bullies choose targets who they think are afraid of them. This strategy works because bullies are usually afraid underneath their apparently tough outsides. They don't bother people who stand up to them.

➽ **If the bully asks you to do something uncomfortable, say no in a calm and clear way.** Never do any thing that makes you feel scared or strange. Tell the bully no in a clear way, and try to act calm and confident, if you can.

➽ **Make an older friend.** Befriend a person who is successful at standing up to bullies. If you have an older sibling, you could ask him or her to help you. You can also ask your teachers to be paired with another student, perhaps an older student,who can help you navigate your school. Older kids are really helpful because people in your grade will listen to them!

➽ **If the bullying gets excessive, tell a trusted adult, such as your parents or teachers.** Your teachers or parents can coach you about how you should respond to the bully. For example, they can help you practice how to act confident or how to ignore the bully at first.

However, if the bullying gets to be too much, you may have to take more serious actions. How do you know when enough is enough? If you feel scared that someone is going to hurt you or has already hurt you, or if you feel sad or worried about going to school because of bullies, it's time for you to trust an adult and let her know what is happening.

You may feel reluctant to tell an adult that another kid is bullying you because this kid may also sometimes act like your friend. However, a true friend does not threaten you or hurt you. Even if you sometimes like to be around another person, he is not your friend if he

> The best way to stand up to a bully is to show him that you aren't scared. Don't react with fear, panic, or anger, if possible.

> If you are being bullied, it's critical to seek help from a trusted adult in private, without the bullies around.

hurts you or insults you. Some kids may even bully other kids without realizing that what they are doing is wrong.

Many states have even passed laws that make it criminal for teachers and school principals to ignore bullying. It is their job to stop bullies. Remember, bullying is wrong, and it is often illegal.

 ## PUT YOUR KNOW-HOW TO WORK

Practice Answering Bullies
What would you say to an older boy who hangs out in the hallways between classes and makes fun of the younger kids? He has come close to your locker and calls you a baby for having a picture of your dog hung up in your locker.

What would you do in this situation?

_____ .

Here are some ideas you could try:

➤ Tell him to stop bothering you by saying, "I'm not afraid of you. Move on."

➤ Ignore the bully, if he doesn't repeat the action.

➤ Tell him that your dog is really cute, so that's why you hang her picture in your locker.

➤ Tell a teacher privately, if the bullying doesn't stop. (But don't tell the boy you are telling the teacher.)

➤ Ask an older friend to stand up for you.

If these ideas don't work to stop the bullying, talk to a trusted adult.

UNDERSTANDING LESS OBVIOUS BULLIES AND MEAN KIDS

Often, it is more difficult to stop sneakier kinds of bullies. These are the kinds of kids who do not throw punches or threaten you with physical violence, but who may try to gossip about you, make fun of you, or lie to you. This person tries to get friends by telling stories about other kids. Sometimes, these stories aren't true. You should try to avoid this type of person, and don't believe everything she says. In other words, take what these kids say with a **grain of salt**.

take with a grain of salt
an expression that means that you should evaluate something that is said and see if it's really true.

PUT YOUR KNOW-HOW TO WORK

Role Play
Practice this situation with a friend, teacher, or parent. Here is the scenario, or set-up for the role play: A kid in your class lies and blames you for ripping up a paper when the teacher stepped out of class. Practice telling the teacher that you didn't rip up the paper. It's up to you whether you tell the teacher who ripped up the paper. Remember to remain calm and clear, and avoid personal attacks and name-calling.

QUESTIONING PEOPLE'S MOTIVES

Often, when people ask you to do something, they have a **motive** or goal in mind that may not be obvious. It is obvious, for example, that when someone asks you for your homework, she wants to copy it and get a good grade. The reasons why people ask for other things are less obvious. Say, for example, that someone says that they want to bet you money that a certain team will win a sports game, and the person asks you for money. He even promises you that you could win a lot of money if your team wins. Here are the questions you should ask yourself in this situation:

motive:
a goal someone has in mind when they say or do something.

➽ Why is the person asking me to give him money?

➽ What does he expect to gain?

➽ Is this person really my friend? Has he been mean to me before, or has he usually been nice to me in the past?

➽ How well do I know this person? If I haven't known him for very long, it's better not to trust him.

deduce:
to figure something out or reach a conclusion.

You should probably **deduce**, or figure out, that often, a person who wants to make a bet is hoping to keep your money, whether or not you win. If you really want to make a bet, make it a gentleman's or lady's bet, which does not involve putting down any money.

In a way, figuring out people's motives is kind of like figuring out the clues to a mystery. There's a great novel called *The Curious Incident of the Dog in the Night-time* by Christopher Haddon (you can get a copy from your library) in which a boy with autism tries to guess his dad's and neighbors' motives as if he were a great detective like Sherlock Holmes. If you read this book, you will learn some new techniques for gathering clues about people's motives, or understanding why they do what they do. People sometimes lie to get out of trouble or to make themselves seem cool in front of other people. You should keep in mind that people, especially those you don't know very well, can have bad motives for doing things.

Here is an example of how you can say no to someone you suspect has bad motives:

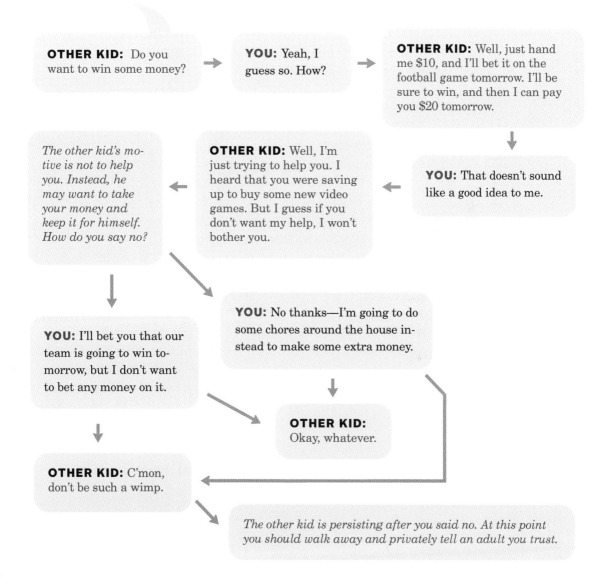

OTHER KID: Do you want to win some money?

YOU: Yeah, I guess so. How?

OTHER KID: Well, just hand me $10, and I'll bet it on the football game tomorrow. I'll be sure to win, and then I can pay you $20 tomorrow.

YOU: That doesn't sound like a good idea to me.

OTHER KID: Well, I'm just trying to help you. I heard that you were saving up to buy some new video games. But I guess if you don't want my help, I won't bother you.

The other kid's motive is not to help you. Instead, he may want to take your money and keep it for himself. How do you say no?

YOU: No thanks—I'm going to do some chores around the house instead to make some extra money.

YOU: I'll bet you that our team is going to win tomorrow, but I don't want to bet any money on it.

OTHER KID: Okay, whatever.

OTHER KID: C'mon, don't be such a wimp.

The other kid is persisting after you said no. At this point you should walk away and privately tell an adult you trust.

Deduce Other Kids' Motives

See if you can figure out what people's motivations are for these kinds of common actions:

1. A kid insults you or another classmate. What is his motivation?

_____.

(Could it be to make himself feel cool by putting someone down, or to make other people afraid of him so he can boss them around?)

2. A kid draws a mean picture on the blackboard. When the teacher enters the room, she asks the kid if he drew the picture, but the kid lies and says no. What is the kid's motivation?

_____.

(The kid clearly wants to avoid getting in trouble by blaming someone else. If he blames you, you should stand up for yourself.)

3. A kid claims that you said something mean about aother kid, even though you didn't. What is the first kid's motivation?

_____.

(The kid who is lying may want to make friends with the kid she lies to. Maybe by telling the other kid a lie, the first kid can pretend that you are not her friend. In this case, you have to tell the second kid that you never said the mean thing, and then, it's up to the kid to believe you.)

4. A kid says that she went on a great vacation to Disney World, even though you know that she stayed at home. What is the kid's motivation to lie in this case?

_____.

(Sometimes, kids like to lie to pretend they have a better life than they do or to make others feel jealous. In this case, their lie isn't really hurting anyone but themselves. Your first response in this situation might be to change the subject or ignore the lie if you think it will make the other kid feel embarrassed. If she constantly lies, you can tell her that you know she is lying, but if she insists on the lie, there isn't much you can do.)

HOW TO UNCOVER FAKE FRIENDS

Sometimes, it's confusing to tell when people are really our friends, or when they are just acting nice because they want something from us—whether it's money, attention, or the opportunity to make fun of us. Here are some questions you can ask yourself about people to determine whether they are real or fake friends:

Real friends are people who:

➤ make us feel good about ourselves

➤ compliment us

➤ tell us the truth

➤ may ask for a favor but also do favors in return

➤ do not make fun of us, except maybe gently

➤ accept "no" as an answer

Bad or fake friends are people who:

➤ ask us for a lot of favors, such as lending them toys or homework, without doing much for us in return

➤ make fun of us

➤ try to make us feel bad about ourselves

➤ laugh at us in a mean way

➤ insult us

➤ tell us lies

➤ don't accept "no" as an answer

➤ hurt us physically, or try to do so.

PUT YOUR KNOW-HOW TO WORK

Evaluate Your Friends
It's time to think about your friends and check them out.
How well would each of your friends do on the following test?

- My friend does not make fun of me.

- My friend sometimes asks me for favors, but she does favors for me too, like lending me things.

- My friend comes over to my house sometimes, and we have a good time.

- My friend does not make fun of other kids or teachers.

- My friend does not do anything that makes me feel uncomfortable.

- I don't feel the need to make fun of other people or make bad jokes when I am with my friend.

How well do your friends do on this test? If your friends don't pass this test, meaning that they aren't like the good friend described on this list, you can do one of the following:

- Talk to your friend about what a true friend is like.

- Consider limiting your time with this person.

- Try to do something else with this person. For example, instead of spending time making fun of other people, suggest that you watch a movie or play video games.

You may think that just because someone eats lunch with you or spends time with you, he is your friend. However, as you can see from the list above, true friends make us feel good about ourselves. *Do not confuse spending time with someone with having a true friendship.* When you are choosing friends, pick people who have qualities from the list of true friends, not the list of bad or fake friends.

STAYING SAFE ONLINE

Bullies can also use computers, the internet, cell phones, and other means to harass people. You may be very good at using computers and understanding applications. However, you should also understand that people you don't know and can't see can threaten you via electronic means. While you can continue enjoying computer games and messaging systems, there are some ideas that you should keep in mind while in cyberspace:

1. Saying something online is not the same as saying it in person. If you send or receive a mean or threatening e-mail or text message, it could present a very serious situation. You never want to send anything mean, threatening, personal, or **defamatory** electronically—period. These kinds of messages could get you in serious hot water (meaning trouble). At the least, they could hurt your friendship with other people; at worst, they could get you in trouble with your parents or with your school.

2. Never post personal information online about yourself or anyone else. Personal information, such as your address, social security number, age, parents' names, siblings' names, etc. can be used against you by people who want access to your house, parents' bank accounts, or other private information. Never share this information with anyone who asks via e-mail, text, chat room, instant message, or Facebook. If you are entering your parents' credit card information online, be sure to do so with your parents present.

3. Set privacy settings on Facebook, Google, and other sites. You can set the privacy settings so that other users don't know you are on Facebook and so that you don't show up in search results.

4. Beware of social media. Sites like Facebook can be great for keeping up with friends, but often, you will receive friend requests from

True friends make you feel good about yourself. A friend who spends time with you but who makes you feel bad about yourself is not a true friend.

defamatory: hurting another person's reputation.

people you don't know. Be careful of friending people you don't know, and don't make personal posts that tell people things they shouldn't know. For example, don't post messages on Facebook that tell people you are going on vacation, as people will know no one is home and may break into your house. This is unlikely to happen, but it's better to be safe and not post this information online.

In addition, be careful of chatting or sending messages to people you don't know. They may ask you for personal information, but do not respond. If you are ever worried about what someone online wants from you or you mistrust the person's motives, tell a trusted adult, such as your parents or a teacher.

Never share the following types of information online:

➤➤ any information about credit cards or your parents' money

➤➤ any information about where you live

➤➤ any information about where your parents work

➤➤ any information about where you go to school

➤➤ any information about your age

> A lot of bullying is carried out online, but you can protect yourself by establishing privacy settings and not giving out any personal information online.

Ask your parents or a trusted adult if you come across these types of messages.

5. Report mean texts or messages, and never send these types of messages. Even if you think people are trying to be funny, these types of messages can be thought of as bullying or even crimes. Do not send these messages, as they can get you in trouble with friends, teachers, parents, and your school principal. Schools have passed laws so that mean messages can result in discipline or punishment, so report any mean messages you receive, and do not put anything mean into a text or other kind of electronic message.

PUT YOUR KNOW-HOW TO WORK

Solve a Mystery

Can you guess why saying the things below might lead to bad results or get you in trouble, particularly if you say these things to people you don't know very well or to people online through chat rooms, e-mails, or Facebook?

➤➤ My family is going away for a week on vacation.

_____

_____

_____.

(This might be dangerous because then people who could rob you will know you will be away. You can tell friends you know well that you are going away, however.)

➤➤ My mom and dad fought.

_____

_____

_____.

(Your parents will not want other people to know that they had a private argument, which sometimes occurs between married people. You should keep this information private.)

➤➤ My brother takes medication for ADHD.

_____

_____

_____.

(Your brother may not want people to know that he has an issue like ADHD, or Attention-Deficit Hyperactivity Disorder. Let him tell people he has this issue if he chooses to.)

➤➤ My mom put a lot of money in the bank today. Her receipt said she had lots of money in her account.

next page

_____

_____

_____.

(Your parents would like you to keep information about the family's money situation private. It is better if people outside the family don't know about your family's money so that they can't take advantage of you.)

You should also not answer any question about money or credit cards online, and, if you should receive that type of message, it is likely from a bad company that is trying to steal from you, rather than from a company that needs this information because you are ordering something from them. Be sure to show these messages to your parents, and do not answer them.

GOAL SETTING:
BULLIES, MEAN KIDS, AND CYBER-SAFETY RULES

Now that you've read the rules about standing up to bullies, write down some goals that you have. Make your goals SMART: that is, Specific, Measurable, Attainable, Realistic, and Timely. For example, here are some goals you might work towards:

➤ This week, I will make sure my privacy settings are established on the major e-mail and internet programs I use, including online games.

➤ I will practice with a friend or adult what I would say if I were threatened by a bully or insulted by another kid.

➤ If I think someone is being unfair to me, I will use the strategies I practiced to stand up for myself.

➤ I will role-play with a friend or adult how I would answer an adult I don't know who asked me for private information, such as my address.

In this chapter, you learned ways to handle bullies. In the next chapter, you will learn some strategies to keep yourself healthy and energized.

CHAPTER 8

HEALTHY HABITS

Part of doing well in school is treating your body well. If you have a healthy body—and you are well-rested and well-nourished—you will be better able to concentrate and do your schoolwork. Feeling tired can make you more likely to feel stressed out.

There is no one way to get healthy, and you can choose the best ways to make yourself feel better—ways that work with what you like to do. You can find the exercise that you like best—whether it's riding horses, hiking, or running. And if you find yourself not liking a lot of foods because of their strange textures or smells, that's all right, too. Just find some options that you like, and try to eat fruit and vegetables that taste good to you.

The better you treat your body, the better it will treat you. If you give your body exercise, relaxation, and the right food, you will feel more energized and less stressed out.

TEST YOURSELF:
How Well Do You Treat Your Body?

1. On a regular basis, I:
__a. Go to bed late, and I feel tired during the day.
__b. I try to get to bed, but I can't fall asleep.
__c. I get at least eight hours of sleep a night.

2. For breakfast, I eat:
__a. Something sweet, or nothing at all.
__b. A piece of bread or toast.
__c. Some cereal and fruit or juice.

3. When I feel really stressed, I:
__a. Play video games.
__b. Don't know what to do.
__c. Take a walk or talk to someone.

4. To keep fit, I:
__a. Don't exercise outside of gym class.
__b. Try to walk around the neighborhood.
__c. Exercise by doing an activity I enjoy.

5. In terms of hygiene, I:
__a. Sometimes forget to bathe.
__b. Usually bathe, but forget to wear deodorant.

__c. Bathe, brush my teeth, and wear deodorant regularly.

6. When I am dressing for school, I:
  __a. Roll out of bed and go to the bus.
  __b. Pull on whatever clothes I have lying around, as long as
      they don't smell too bad.
  __c. Put on the outfit I planned out the night before.

If you answered mostly "a," you may feel better if you read this chapter to figure out ways to relax, eat right, and get some exercise. These strategies may help you feel more relaxed and, at the same time, more energized and alert.

If you answered mostly "b," you understand the importance of eating right, sleeping, and getting exercise, which is great. You may need some ideas from this chapter about how to achieve these goals.

If you answered mostly "c," you are doing a good job of reducing your stress levels by exercising, sleeping, and eating right, and you know how to take care of your body. Read on to find some potentially new ideas about how to stay healthy.

GETTING ENOUGH SLEEP

It's vital to get enough sleep each night, and, if you don't, you will likely feel crabby. If you don't sleep enough over time, you may find that you are feeling very stressed or unable to do your work.

Some people with Asperger's struggle with sleeping because they have a lot of worries, which is natural and understandable. If you have a lot of worries, read the section in Chapter 2 on understanding and dealing with your fears. It may give you some ideas about how to put your worries aside or reduce your worrying on a daily level.

GOOD PRE-SLEEP ROUTINES

To get a good night's sleep, it is important to have a good pre-sleep routine. Try to do the following each night:

➤ Turn off electronic devices, such as televisions, computers, and video games, at least an hour before bed.

➤ Turn off loud music and overhead lights.

➤ Go to bed each night at the same time, and try to get up at the usual time, even on the weekends.

If you are usually really tired after school, take a twenty-minute nap when you get home from school. Avoid taking longer naps that will interfere with your regular bedtime. Try not to do homework right before bed, which will engage your mind and may keep you awake.

RELAXATION TECHNIQUES

If you are finding it hard to get to sleep, you may need to practice a **relaxation technique**, which is a way to calm your mind and body. Try some of the following strategies:

➤ Concentrate on your breathing. Take a deep breath and breathe out slowly while putting your hand on your belly and feeling your lungs empty.

➤ Exercise is the best way to feel relaxed and ready for sleep. Try to exercise earlier in the day, not right before bed, and find an activity that you enjoy—whether it's taking a brisk walk, working out in the gym, hiking, horseback riding, or doing yoga.

➤ Try **progressive muscle relaxation.** Sit for a few minutes with your eyes closed, while tensing and then relaxing each part of your body. Start with the tips of your toes and focus on relaxing each part of your body.

➤ Try thinking about anything that is bothering you. Write down some of your thoughts for a few minutes, and try to clear your head of them.

➤ Give yourself ten minutes to think about your worries and

Turning off your electronic devices an hour before bed gives your eyes and brain a rest.

If you like to read before bed, try using a bedside lamp or a book light instead of bright, overhead lights.

This helps your body get used to the same sleep schedule.

relaxation technique:
a way to calm your body and mind.

Exercise is also a great way to defeat anxiety and feel less stressed.

progressive muscle relaxation:
a way to relax by tensing and then relaxing each part of your body.

Writing down your thoughts in a journal can help relieve your worries. Express yourself and clear your mind.

then decide that it is time to put them aside for the day.

➤ Take a warm shower or bath before bed.

➤ Read a book in bed.

➤ Listen to relaxing, calm music or a book on CD.

Finally, if sleep remains a problem, ask your parents to talk to your doctor for some additional help.

EATING WELL

Just as a car must have the right level of octane fuel to run well, your body must have the right food to make it run well. You can fill yourself with junk food, but you will find that junk food, like low-grade fuel in a car's engine, will eventually cause your body to break down. If you give yourself sufficient fuel, you will feel more energized to take on the day and complete everything you need to do.

You may find that certain foods don't taste good or that particular textures bother you, and you are, within your parents' rules, allowed to choose the foods you like. Although you may have certain foods you dislike, try to follow these rules:

➤ Eat a well-balanced diet that includes fruits, vegetables, healthy meats such as chicken and fish, and whole grains.

➤ Eat regularly. That means you should eat a full breakfast with items such as cereal, toast, juice, fruit, or yogurt. If you don't eat breakfast, you may feel burned out or tired before you even get to lunch. Eating right is particularly important if you have a busy or stressful day at school with tests or other events.

➤ If you can't eat right when you get up, try to bring some nutrtious food, such as yogurt or toast with peanut butter, to school with you to eat before the day begins.

➤ Limit junk food, such as fast food, donuts, cookies, candy, and other foods that don't have much nutritional value.

➤ If you are interested, read the nutrition labels on food to understand how much fat or salt (usually called sodium on food labels) a food contains. You will most likely become very good at understanding what kinds of nutrients are in food and will get better at picking more nutritious foods over time.

PUT YOUR KNOW-HOW TO WORK

Rate Your Meals
Rate how healthy the following meals are, using *healthy, sort of healthy,* or *unhealthy.*

1. A breakfast of a donut, orange juice, and cookies.

_____

2. A lunch of a chicken sandwich, fries, and a soft drink.

_____

3. A dinner of a tossed salad, whole-wheat spaghetti, turkey meat balls, and some milk.

_____

Answers: 1) This is an unhealthy meal, except for the orange juice. It won't give you energy for the day, and it won't be very good for your body or your teeth! 2) This meal is sort of healthy—chicken is a healthy meat and better for you than a hamburger. Swap out green beans for the fries, and drink natural juice or milk instead of soda. You will have a lot more energy for your day! 3) This is a healthy meal, and one that will help you feel good. You have veggies, healthy meat like turkey, and whole-wheat rather than white spaghetti. Non-fat milk is good for your bones, too.

If you find that you have a hard time trying new foods, you may want to sample new foods one by one. Try to figure out which textures you like; for example, you may prefer smooth textures like pudding or applesauce, or you may prefer crunchier textures like apples and popcorn. Bring healthy foods into your diet that have these textures. For example, if you like smooth textures, you can have a fruit smoothie instead of eating whole fruits. Even though the food is in a different form, it is still healthy for you. If you are having a hard time finding nutritious foods that you like, speak to your school nurse or doctor. They might be able to recommend a nutritious plan for you or find someone called a nutritionist to help you.

HAVING GOOD HYGIENE

Just as car owners must make sure that their vehicles are shiny and clean, you own your body and are responsible for your hygiene. When you go to school, the other kids and teachers expect that you will have done the following:

➡ Brushed your teeth well each morning and night. If you don't, your teeth will be in bad shape, and you may have bad breath. It's hard to speak with someone with bad breath, so be sure to brush all over your mouth and tongue for at least two minutes each morning and two minutes every night before bed.

➡ Taken a shower each morning or at night before bed. Showering each day is especially important if it's hot out or if you've done physical activities that make you sweaty or smelly.

➡ Used a deodorant under both arm pits to prevent you from smelling. You should ask your parents to buy you a deodorant that has anti-perspirant to prevent you from sweating in school.

➡ Brushed your hair so that it looks relatively neat.

➡ Dressed yourself so that you are wearing clean clothes that match and socks that match.

See the section "Getting Dressed" on page 122, if you'd like more information about how to dress better or how to style your hair.

PUT YOUR KNOW-HOW TO WORK

Rate Your Habits
Rate yourself on how well you do the following.

1. I brush my teeth every morning and night.
a) Yes, always
b) Sometimes
c) Rarely
d) Not sure

2. I eat a well-balanced breakfast with fruit and cereal or yogurt or other nutritious foods such as eggs.
a) Yes, always
b) Sometimes
c) Rarely
d) Not sure

3. I am able to relax at night.
a) Yes, always
b) Sometimes
c) Rarely
d) Not sure

4. I do regular exercise to stay fit.
a) Yes, always
b) Sometimes
c) Rarely
d) Not sure

5. I eat fruits and vegetables every day.
a) Yes, always
b) Sometimes
c) Rarely
d) Not sure

If you answered mostly "Rarely" or "Not sure," don't worry. You can turn these items into some of your goals at the end of the chapter.

GETTING DRESSED

hygiene:
how to take care
of your body.

In addition to practicing good **hygiene**, dressing well and styling your hair in a way that looks good on you can help you feel good about yourself and fit in better at school.

You can dress any way you like, as long as you follow your school's and parents' rules. You should dress in a way that makes you the most comfortable, particularly if you are bothered by scratchy fabrics or tags. Before you get dressed for school, check that your clothes are clean and not too wrinkled. It may be helpful to plan your outfits the night before, so you will be able to get dressed quickly in the morning.

Dressing well
can help you
feel good about
yourself.

You may choose, however, to dress the way other people in your school do, at least in some ways. Dressing the way the other kids do is kind of like the way an animal uses camouflage. If you dress at least a bit like other kids, you will blend in more and be freer to do what you want. Notice what the other kids are wearing. Do they all tend to wear the same kinds of jeans or shirts or sneakers? If so, **make a mental note** about what they are wearing.

make a mental note:
pay attention to something so that you will remember it later.

You can also look at magazines geared to teenagers to discover the latest styles. You don't have to spend a lot of money getting new clothes. You can visit a thrift or vintage store or a discount store. If you think your hair needs some work, visit your hair stylist and ask him or her to work on a hairstyle that flatters your face. Ask your stylist about tips for getting your hair to look good each morning.

PUT YOUR KNOW-HOW TO WORK

Get Dressed for School

Before leaving for school in the morning, ask yourself if you've done each of the steps in this checklist:

☐ Did I brush my teeth?

☐ Did I shower/bathe in the morning or the night before?

☐ Did I wash my hair in the shower?

☐ Did I put on deodorant (under my arms)?

☐ Do my socks match?

☐ Do my shirt and pants match?

☐ Are my clothes clean?

☐ Did I bring additional clothes for gym or another activity?

☐ Are my clothes wrinkled?

☐ Did I comb my hair?

GOAL SETTING:

HEALTHY HABITS RULES

Now that you've digested (do you notice the pun here and the double meaning of digesting food and digesting information?) the rules about healthy habits, write down some goals that you have. Make your goals SMART: that is, Specific, Measurable, Attainable, Realistic, and Timely. For example, here are some goals you might work towards:

➤ I will try to eat a nutritious breakfast each morning with fruit juice, cereal, and toast.

➤ I will try to run twice a week.

➤ I will work on turning off my computers and video games at 9pm before my bedtime at 10pm.

In this chapter, you learned ways to keep yourself well and rested. Read on to find some websites, books, and games that can offer you more information about Asperger's and how to understand the rules of school.

RESOURCES

Websites, Books, and Games
(Yes, Games!) to Help You

WEBSITES

OASIS:
http://www.aspergersyndrome.org/
A website with information and support for people with Asperger's. The website allows you to search for local support groups and other resources, and there are also articles about Asperger's. OASIS also has a handy teacher's guide that you and your parents can give to your teacher to provide him with a bit of background and information about how to help you in the classroom.

Your Little Professor:
http://www.yourlittleprofessor.com/resources.html
This website lists support groups and other resources for people with Asperger's and their families, and there are helpful articles on the site about friendships, bullying, and the gifts of Asperger's.

Wrong Planet:
http://www.wrongplanet.net
This website is an online community for people with Asperger's and their families. There is a discussion forum and a chat room for people to interact. Be sure to ask your parents' permission before you post on this site.

BOOKS

All Cats Have Asperger Syndrome
by Kathy Hoopmann (Jessica Kingsley, 2006).
A great book that helps explain Asperger's using cats. There are some wonderful cat photos, and this book is perfect for pet lovers.

Can I Tell You About Asperger Syndrome?: A Guide for Friends and Family
by Jude Welton (Jessica Kingsley, 2003).
This book is told from the point of view of a boy named Adam, who has Asperger's. Adam explains to other people what Asperger's is and how it feels to have Asperger's. This short book is easy and quick to read, and it can help other people understand Asperger's better.

The Curious Incident of the Dog in the Night-time
by Mark Haddon (Vintage, 2004).
This is an interesting account of how a 15-year-old boy with autism tries to solve the mystery of who killed the neighbor's dog. The main character is able to use his sense of logic to unlock the mystery.

Diagnosing Jefferson
by Norm Ledgin (Future Horizons, 2000).
The author writes about how Thomas Jefferson, a former U.S. president and an inventor, may have had Asperger's syndrome, leading to his remarkable abilities.

Look Me in the Eye: My Life with Asperger's
by John Elder Robison (Broadway, 2008).
The author writes in a humorous way about his childhood with Asperger's syndrome and his later adult life, during which he designed rocket-like guitars for rock bands and started a successful business fixing expensive cars.

Thinking in Pictures: My Life with Autism
by Temple Grandin (Vintage, 2010).
In this book, the author—now a famous animal scientist who lectures people around the country on animal treatment and behavior and about what it's like to live with autism—talks about her life and those of others affected by autism. Though autism isn't exactly the same as Asperger's, it's another situation that can make it difficult for people to communicate and understand others, and the author of this book talks about subjects that relate to people with Asperger's.

GAMES

Whiz Kid Games:
http://www.whizkidgames.com/
Free online games that help you understand people's facial expressions and help you deal with change.

ABOUT THE AUTHOR

Blythe Grossberg, PsyD, is a learning specialist in New York City who specializes in helping children with Asperger's syndrome and learning issues become more effective at school. She has worked for over a decade with middle and high school students with learning issues, such as ADD, language and reading disorders, spatial and math disorders, Asperger's syndrome, and others, to help them get organized, succeed in school, and perform on standardized tests. Dr. Grossberg is the author of *Making ADD Work: On-the-job Strategies for Coping with Attention Deficit Disorder, Test Success: Test-Taking and Study Strategies for All Students, Including Those with ADD and LD*, and *Applying to College for Students with ADD or LD*. A graduate of Harvard College and Rutgers Graduate School of Applied and Professional Psychology, she has written for *ADDitude Magazine, New York Times* supplements, and other publications. She has spoken before the Manhattan Adult ADD Support Group and CHADD (Children and Adults with ADD). Her work has also been featured on ADDManagement.com and other websites for people with ADD. She is also the private school guide for About.com.

ABOUT MAGINATION PRESS

Magination Press publishes self-help books for kids and the adults in their lives. Magination Press is an imprint of the American Psychological Association, the largest scientific and professional organization representing psychologists in the United States and the largest association of psychologists worldwide.